CRITIC AT LARGE

PREVIOUS BOOKS BY D.J. TAYLOR

Non-fiction

A Vain Conceit: British Fiction in the 1980s

Other People: Portraits from the '90s (with Marcus Berkmann)

After the War: The Novel and England Since 1945

Thackeray

Orwell: The Life

On the Corinthian Spirit: The Decline of Amateurism in Sport

Bright Young People: The Rise and Fall of a Generation 1918–1940

What You Didn't Miss: A Book of Literary Parodies

The New Book of Snobs

The Prose Factory: Literary Life in England Since 1918

Lost Girls: Love, War and Literature 1939–1951

On Nineteen Eighty-Four: A Biography

Fiction

Great Eastern Land

Real Life

English Settlement

After Bathing at Baxter's: Stories

Trespass

The Comedy Man

Kept: A Victorian Mystery

Ask Alice

At the Chime of a City Clock

Derby Day

Secondhand Daylight

The Windsor Faction

From the Heart (Amazon Kindle Single)

Wrote for Luck: Stories

Rock and Roll is Life

Stewkey Blues: Stories

CRITIC AT LARGE

Essays and Reviews: 2010–2022

D.J. Taylor

Printed by imprintdigital
Upton Pyne, Exeter
www.digital.imprint.co.uk

Typesetting and cover design by The Book Typesetters
hello@thebooktypesetters.com
07422 598 168
www.thebooktypesetters.com

Published by Shoestring Press
19 Devonshire Avenue, Beeston, Nottingham, NG9 1BS
(0115) 925 1827
www.shoestringpress.co.uk

First published 2023
© Copyright: D.J. Taylor
© Cover painting/photograph:

The moral right of the author has been asserted.

ISBN 978-1-915553-19-5

For J.S. Barnes

CONTENTS

INTRODUCTION

When I started writing literary journalism, I used to keep a cuttings book. Everything went into it: anonymous paragraphs submitted to *Private Eye*; postage stamp-sized reviews for the *London Evening Standard*; incremental steps, I fondly assured myself, on that life-long traipse up Mount Olympus. After a while, as the flow increased – by the early 1990s I was writing three or four pieces a week – I got bored with the cuttings book, or rather books, and resorted to simply snipping the articles out from, as it may have been, the arts sections of the *Sunday Times* or the *New Statesman*, and stowing them away in an outsize cardboard box. After a slightly longer interval, I got bored with doing this and gave up the archival process altogether. Even so, the box still harbours a two-foot high pile of old newspaper which, on the last occasion that I tipped the contents out over the floor to see what might be lurking there, covered the entire carpet of the room in which it was housed.

'Nobody wants to read old book reviews,' Simon Raven once declared when introducing a miscellany entitled *Boys Will be Boys*, mostly composed of old book reviews, back in 1963. As a long-term dweller in what the Victorian novelist George Gissing once called 'the valley of the shadow of books', I have always had a soft spot for this modest and unassuming sub-genre of lit. crit. In fact, the study shelves are crammed with assemblies of this kind: D.J. Enright's wonderfully-titled *Poets and Conspirators*, Brigid Brophy's *Don't Never Forget*, Ian Hamilton's *Walking Possession*, Julian Symons's *Critical Observations*. And this is to ignore such ornaments of Victorian Grub Street as John Churton Collins, the Revd. George Gilfillan and Professor Saintsbury – all those inky-fingered denizens of the Gladstone-era reviews who populate such field-guides to the profession as John Gross's *The Rise and Fall of the Man of Letters* (1969), which, over half-a-century after its first publication seems to me one of the most extraordinary books ever written.

None of this, naturally, is to ignore the faint air of defensiveness that rises over these compilations, born of a suspicion that the book review, as opposed to the critical essay or the scholarly monograph, has a necessarily short shelf-life and in the vast majority of cases were better unpreserved. Even in the 1950s, Cyril Connolly – a critic who spent far too much time agonising over the value of his craft – feared that the role he occupied was heading rapidly to extinction:

> At the opposite end to the university teacher of 'creative writing' is the literary journalist. He cannot afford to be obscure; he is not subsidised; he has to compress his views into a few hundred words; he must grade, explain and entertain all at once, and his work is immediately forgotten, totally ignored except for those who write in to correct a name or a date.

Connolly is over-stating his case, of course, and one of the heartening features of the literary landscape nearly 70 years after he over-stated it, is how tenaciously the freelance reviewer endures and how regularly, in an age where most people are terrified of saying in public what they really feel about anything, there rises from a newspaper arts section or magazine book column the sound of someone declining to follow the party line.

The pieces collected here were all written between 2010 and 2022. They include introductions to reissued books, straightforward reviews, anniversary commemorations and one or two miscellaneous and unclassifiable items which, for convenience's sake, I have filed under 'Enthusiasms.' They were written for a variety of reasons (for a proper *apologia pro vita sua* see the essay 'Why Review Books?') – to prove a point; to pay a bill; to keep my family in the style to which they would like to become accustomed – but, above all, for the pleasure I experienced in writing them. Professor Saintsbury, who reviewed for sixty years, once remarked that even in his eighties his fingers still twitched as he tore open a parcel of books for review. Although two decades younger than the author of *Historical Manual of English Prosody* (1910) when he wrote these words, I feel exactly the same. I am very grateful to John Lucas, who came up with the idea of assembling this collection, and also to the many editorial sponsors who commissioned the original pieces. They include Stig Abell, Mark Amory, James Campbell, Suzi Feay, Tom Fleming, Tom Gatti, Roger Kimball, Paul Laity, Toby Lichtig, Fiona Macmillan, Michael Mosbacher, Ben Riley, Robert Potts, Sameer Rahim, Nancy Sladek, Graham Stewart and Boyd Tonkin. Love and thanks, as ever, to Rachel, Felix, Benjy and Leo.

Grateful acknowledgment is made to *The Critic*, EIS Media, the *Guardian*, *Literary Review*, *The New Criterion*, *New Statesman*, *Prospect*, *The Spectator* and the *Times Literary Supplement*, for permission to reprint copyrighted material

D.J. Taylor
Norwich
24 June 2022

I. PRE-MODERNS

PARALLEL LIVES:
TROLLOPE AND *CAN YOU FORGIVE HER*

Some of the most bracing moments in novels come when a writer decides to use his characters as proxies in a debate about the nature of fiction itself, setting up an argument where what is at stake is not simply two imaginary people's views about aesthetics, but the whole idea of how you go about writing a book in the first place. There is a pointed little scene in Anthony Powell's *The Soldier's Art* (1966), the eighth volume in his *Dance to the Music of Time* sequence, in which Nick Jenkins, out on a night exercise in war-time Ulster, comes across his commanding officer, General Liddament, reading 'a small blue book that had the air of being a pocket edition of some classic.' Having established that the latrines have been correctly sited, the General suddenly raises the volume above his head and asks: what does Jenkins think of Trollope? Taken unawares, the junior officer insists that he has 'never found Trollope easy to read.' 'Why not?' the General demands. Discovering that 'a few worn shreds of long-forgotten literary criticism were just pliant enough to be patched hurriedly together in substitute for a more suitable garment to cover the dialectic nakedness of the statement just made,' Jenkins embarks on a halting and increasingly fragmentary defence of his position:

> '…the style… certain repetitive tricks of phrasing…
> psychology often unconvincing… sometimes downright
> dishonest in treating of individual relationships… women
> don't analyse their own predicaments as there
> represented… in fact, the author does more thinking than
> feeling… of course, possessor of enormous narrative gifts…
> marshalling material… all that amounting to genius…

certain sense of character, even if stylised… and naturally
as a picture of the times…'

All this, however brusquely received ('Rubbish' General
Liddament shoots back), is a rather acute summary of what might
be called the highbrow position on Trollope, a series of criticisms
liable to be brought out at any time over the last century and a
half by such detractors as Henry James (who famously remarked
of *Can You Forgive Her?* 'Of course we can, and forget her, too, for
that matter') and F.R. Leavis, who condemned his entire *oeuvre*
on the strength of a single volume. At its core lies a determination
to convict Trollope of a kind of aesthetic sleight-of-hand, of
affecting to offer a particular view of human behaviour but in the
end, when the moral chips are down, serving up something else
in default, of encouraging the reader to make certain assumptions
about his treatment of people's emotional lives and then declining
to fulfil them, of setting up various psychological and procedural
challenges and then, inexplicably, failing to follow them through.
The darling of the Victorian subscription library, this argument
implies, is not a realist but, that fatal thing, a conventionalist, not
a delineator of individual character but a contriver of endless
variations on the same behavioural theme, not interested in
human quiddity but in a series of repetitive patternings, and
whose most exalted flights are generally brought down to earth by
haute-stylisation. These are serious complaints, and it takes a
novel like *Can You Forgive Her?*, first published in monthly parts
between January 1864 and August 1865, to demonstrate just how
little they matter in any consideration of Trollope's place among
the mid-Victorian classics.

Although it is always regarded as the first instalment of the six-
part 'political' Palliser sequence (the other volumes are *Phineas
Finn,* 1869, *The Eustace Diamonds,* 1873, *Phineas Redux,*1874,
The Prime Minister, 1876, and *The Duke's Children,* 1880) there is
actually relatively little practical politics in *Can You Forgive Her?*
Certainly Plantagenet Palliser, the novel's diffident joint male

lead, turns down the chance of becoming Chancellor of the Exchequer in a reconfigured Liberal government, and there are a number of quiet words discreetly dropped in the presence of ministerial hopefuls, but at its heart lies an immensely skilful variation on one of Trollope's constant themes, in which two intensely felt emotional triangles run on side by side. Alice Vavasour, whom we are invited to forgive, is a girl of limited but independent means, who in the novel's opening chapters is booked to marry a gentlemanly Cambridgeshire scholar named John Grey. However, there are two impediments to this excellent prospect. The first is that Mr Grey, with his lean good looks, his blameless private life, his £1500 a year and his nice little property in the Fens, is too much of a paragon to be borne ("'So that is it?'" Alice's father notes, catching the first faint hint of his daughter's unease. "'He is a shade too good. Well I have always thought that myself. But it is a fault on the right side.'") The second is the renaissance in Alice's affections of her scapegrace cousin George, to whom she was previously engaged, one of those desperate 'wild men' in whom Victorian fiction abounds, quarrelsome and vengeful, who wants her money to finance a seat in parliament. Urged on by George's over-partial sister Kate, and to the horror of various grand relations who have condescended to approve the match, Alice throws over her fiancé and sets about ruining herself on her cousin's behalf.

Meanwhile, the same pattern is in the process of repeating itself several rungs higher up the social ladder. Alice has another grand relation, the former Lady Glencora M'Cluskie, whose vast estates and bank balances have been welded to those enjoyed (at any rate prospectively) by Plantagenet Palliser, a rising young star of the Treasury bench, and nephew and heir of the Duke of Omnium. Here, too, there is a problem, for Mr Palliser is a dry stick, disappointed by the absence of a baby, decently attached to his juvenile wife but shy, proud and undemonstrative and apparently keener on rapt, small-hours study among the blue books than the comforts of the marital bed. Worse, Lady

Glencora's former suitor, the fabulously dissipated Burgo Fitzgerald, whose Byronic good looks mysteriously endure however much cherry brandy he sinks, is scheming to carry her off. Gradually, as Alice is invited to stay at the Pallisers' country house and becomes her cousin's confidante, the two plots start to converge. In each case disaster is only narrowly averted. Lady Glencora confesses to her husband that she came within an inch of abandoning him. Alice's fortune is only preserved by some dextrous subterfuge on the part of Mr Grey, in cahoots with her horrified father. In the end the orthodoxies of the Victorian novel prevail, the damned proceed to perdition and the chosen resume the even tenor of their lives, but, as both Mr Palliser and John Grey reflect to themselves, it has been a very near thing.

On one level, then, *Can You Forgive Her?* is a case-study in knowing your limitations, settling if not for second-best than for security and comfort rather than the lure of the tantalising unknown. It would be perfectly possible, 150 years later, to construct a kind of alternative naturalistic version of it in which a socially ostracised Lady Glencora decamps with Burgo to the Mediterranean olive groves to watch her beloved drink himself to death, while Alice marries George and sits miserably by as he squanders her fortune before trading her in for a younger model. But this, understandably, is a book that Trollope could never have written. Unlike one or two European contemporaries of the Balzac-Zola school, who would have had an instructive time anatomising Burgo's decline or the degradation of George's discarded mistress Jane, he is interested not in social outcasts but in people whose success in life rests on their ability to calibrate their behaviour to the demands of the society of which they are a part.

But having acknowledged that his audience will never permit him to detach Lady Glencora from Mr Palliser, or allow Alice to marry scar-faced, stick-at-nothing George, Trollope is careful to allow nearly every one of his major characters the means of defying our expectations of them. So dry-as-dust Mr Palliser eventually reveals himself as a human being rather than a walking parliamentary act, not merely by putting his wife's interests before his political ambitions but by striking up a mutually sustaining friendship with Grey during the continental tour that sets everything right. George Vavasour, too, is a terrific creation – a man prepared to stop at absolutely nothing, consumed with spite and jealousy, but with an odd, whimsical side, who muses, of the rekindling of his relationship with Alice, that 'If I did it at all… it would be more with the object of cutting him out than anything else', and at one point even finesses his way into Mr Grey's lodgings as he sits at breakfast with the object of putting a bullet in his head. 'What I mean is this' George observes at one point, trying to encapsulate his philosophy of life in a sentence or two, 'that I hold myself in readiness to risk anything at any moment, in order to gain any object that may serve my turn. I am always ready to lead a forlorn hope.'

Significantly, this hankering for psychological realism, of letting people be themselves in so far as it is consistent with the ultimate sanctions of taste, extends even to the comic sub-plot, which follows Kate's progress around Norfolk in the company of her newly-widowed and newly-wealthy aunt. In a burlesqued version of the two more august relationships being conducted among the London drawing-rooms, Aunt Greenow is vigorously pursued by two middle-aged suitors – a penniless yet enticing scamp named Captain Bellfield and the well-heeled but vainglorious farmer Mr Cheesacre ('I don't owe a sixpence to ere a man or ere a company in the world… I'm Samuel Cheesacre of Oileymead, and it's all my own.') A less subtle writer would have turned Mrs Greenow into a caricature, making hay with her late husband's leavings as his corpse grows cold. Trollope, on the other hand, is quick to emphasize that the tears Mrs Greenow sheds over the deceased's unprepossessing portrait are as genuine as her relish of snug little dinners, genteel lodgings in Norwich Cathedral Close and a boy in buttons to open the door to her friends. 'The charm of the woman was in this' he notes, 'that she

11

was never in the least ashamed of anything that she did.' Having had to make her own way in the world, the widow doubles up as generous friend and freelance marriage broker, shrewdly counselling her niece on her chances in the marketplace and, having finally given the nod to one suitor, fixing up her friend Miss Fairstairs with the other.

Mrs Greenow's ability to look after herself, and in particular to tie up her money in such a way that her new husband shan't get his hands on it – this a decade and a half before the passing of the Married Women's Property Act – gestures at another of the novel's themes. For in however quiet and subterranean a way, this is also a study of sexual politics, and mainstream Victorian society's treatment of women who threaten to disrupt a male-ordered world either by taking control of their finances or deciding to please themselves rather than the people around them. Lady Glencora is the greatest heiress in the kingdom and yet on marriage her wealth is instantly transferred to her husband. There is a rather revealing moment when a trouble-making old lady, hired by Mr Palliser to keep an eye on his flighty young wife and mystified by her eagerness to offer Alice a ride home in the carriage, protests that gentlemen don't like their horses being kept out late. They are her horses Glencora snaps back, and she will do as she likes with them. In the same way, Mr Grey's well-meant deception over the transfer of Alice's funds to George is, depending on your point of view, either a noble act of selflessness which rescues a misguided young woman from the consequences of her folly or an unwarranted act of interference in somebody else's life.

The modern reader is quite likely to emerge from *Can You Forgive Her?* with a sneaking suspicion that, however morally satisfying the outcome, one, if not two, of its female characters have had their emotional lives (not to mention their fortunes) quietly manipulated in order to achieve it. Even during the drawn-out finale, when the forces of Lady Glencora, Mr Palliser and John Grey are marshalled against solitary, recalcitrant Alice one sometimes wonders why, if Miss Vavasour has such doubts about her pursuer, she should be more or less coerced into marrying him. Not the least of Trollope's achievements is to seed his series of moral lessons with so many qualifications that there are times when the whole philosophical edifice seems in grave danger of being undermined. A twenty-first century F.R. Leavis would probably complain that Alice Vavasour would work better as an Emma Bovary, prepared to sacrifice almost anything to satisfy her innermost desires. Trollope would probably reply that ninety-nine per cent of human life is not like that. He might also point out that this ninety-nine per cent can be a great deal more complex and a great deal less straightforward in its motivation than it sometimes appears.

Introduction to Vintage Classics edition of Can You Forgive Her, *2011*

THE LAST VICTORIAN:
GEORGE GISSING AND *THE WHIRLPOOL*

In the early summer of 1896, hard at work on the manuscript of what was to become *The Whirlpool*, George Gissing struck up a connection with the Jewish novelist Israel Zangwill. A natural solitary, wary of unburdening himself even to the friendliest male associate, Gissing seems to have decided that Zangwill, author of the best-selling *Children of the Ghetto*, was a suitable repository for his confidence. The fascinated account that Zangwill gave to his friend Montagu Elder of the evening on which Gissing 'poured out his sad soul' offers a horribly accurate *precis* of some of the personal demons that threatened to drag him down.

> He is a handsome youthful chap but seems to have bungled
> his life in every possible way, and after a terrible uphill fight
> to be still burdened with some woman who, I suspect,
> breaks out in drink. He hates woman and is not in love
> with life. From another source I hear that the cloud on his
> career had its origin in imprisonment for stealing money
> from overcoats &c when he was the pride of Owen's
> College, Manchester…

Above the miseries that Gissing brought upon himself in a career that stretched back to the early 1880s there rises the unmistakable scent of fatalism. His first wife, a prostitute whom he imagined he could redeem, and for whose benefit he was reduced to thieving from his fellow students, was already dead in conditions of unimaginable squalor; her replacement – a working-class girl named Edith Underwood, more or less picked up in the street – had spent the four years of their marriage making his existence hell. In fact the domestic background against which *The Whirlpool* was written, mostly between May and December 1896, is a pattern demonstration of this shy and hyper-sensitive man's habit of strewing his path through life with the kind of self-made obstacles calculated to impede his progress. By early 1896 the family Gissing – father, mother and four-year-old son Walter – had been quartered at Epsom for nearly two years. The arrival of a second child, Alfred, soured Edith's temperament to the point where Gissing resolved to transfer Walter to the care of his aunts in Wakefield. The separation produced a letter from mother to son signed off 'with much love and kisses'. This Walter silently decorated with a drawing of a woman holding a stick.

Naturally all these afflictions wrought a physical effect. A photograph taken in the spring of 1896 shows a ravaged, unhappy-looking man – 'shockingly haggard and aged beyond his thirty-nine years' as one of his biographers puts it. He took a short holiday in a picturesque part of North Wales – much of the scenery reappears in *The Whirlpool*'s central section – and in the intervals of canvassing sympathetic friends on Walter's plight ('I am responsible for his future, and I *know* I am doing the right – the only right – thing'), his dealings with Edith kept to a bare minimum and the study door firmly shut, settled down to write. Progress was unexpectedly rapid. On 9 May he was able to inform his friend Eduard Bertz that 'I have got to work again, quite seriously, and have done *three chapters* of my new book'. There were more domestic upheavals, sparked by Edith's habit of conducting shouting matches with the servants, but after a family holiday at the end of July, Gissing was back in the routine of his eight-hour working days: most of *The Whirlpool*'s 180,000 words were written by the middle of December. If this should seem an extraordinary rate of production, even by late-Victorian standards, then *New Grub Street* (1891) had been finished in a bare six weeks.

In the letter to Bertz, Gissing notes that 'the theme is the decay of domestic life among certain classes of people, and much stress is laid upon the question of *children*'. But while there are several gloom-laden aphorisms on the inadvisability of marriage, and some poignant scenes that clearly reflect Gissing's attachment to his elder son, very little of *The Whirlpool* is straightforwardly autobiographical, if only because it is set in a social sphere several rungs above the one which Gissing himself inhabited. As such it belongs to the second, or even third phase of his career. Gissing's early novels are essentially pieces of slum reportage. The clutch that followed them, notably *New Grub Street* (1891) and *Born in Exile* (1892), are largely about humbly born but intellectual types trying ineffectually to tug free from the shackles that constrain them, a task rendered doubly dangerous by its social dimension. From the angle of the late-Victorian reviewer, *The Whirlpool* is outwardly a more conventional work: a story of middle-class manners, and middle-class morals, with a hero to match. Diffident Harvey Rolfe, with his £900 a year – twice as much as Gissing was earning throughout most of the 1890s – and his library full of books is not so much Gissing himself as the person that Gissing wanted to be, and the upper-bourgeois world whose margins he laconically treads is clearly one that his creator knew only at a distance. There is, consequently, something rather self-conscious about the paraphernalia of the novel's drawing-room scenes, its string quartets on genteel display, and its accounts of society – even society of a rather questionable kind – in action, the thought of newspaper gossip columns and musical gazetteers being robbed for supporting detail.

On the other hand it would be a mistake to assume that Gissing was ignorant of the world on which he sardonically reports. Rather, his absorption in late-Victorian social life is a mark of his artistic conscientiousness, his determination to tether his characters to the world of which he imagined them to be a part, and his interest in how much money a 'lady' might spend in keeping up her wardrobe in 1886, the year in which the novel is set, stems from the same impulse that led him to file the forensic reports on how to live miserably on nothing a year that are such a feature of *The Odd Women* (1893). At the same time, the world in which *The Whirlpool* is established – the world of gentlemen's clubs, West End bun-fights and private incomes – offers a perfect vehicle for some of the anxieties he had begun to cultivate about the moral direction of late-Victorian life and its effect on the individual sensibilities gathered up in its slipstream. G. K. Chesterton once said that nearly every writer will at some point in his career produce a book whose title sums up his attitude to life. Dickens's, naturally, was *Great Expectations*; Scott's *Tales of a Grandfather*. Judged by this yardstick, Gissing's is *Born in Exile* – a phrase that all too faithfully conveys his sense of having been detached by circumstance from the life he most wanted to lead – but *The Whirlpool*, with its homilies on the precariousness of human existence, the constant danger of being swept away into a maelstrom from which there is no return, runs it a very close second. Unusually for Gissing, who generally avoids prompt cards of this kind, the words of the title echo through the book. At an early stage in the proceedings Rolfe assures his friend Hugh Carnaby that he feels 'as if we were all being swept into a ghastly whirlpool which roars over the bottomless pit'. Later on his wife refers half-jokily to their rented house at Pinner, a convenient 30-minute train-ride from the West End, as being 'on the outer edge of the whirlpool'. When Rolfe makes the unwelcome discovery that for the first time in his life he has financial cares to worry him he talks immediately of 'being drawn into the whirlpool'. Finally there is a dramatic exchange between Carnaby and Rolfe, after the former has accidentally killed a man he wrongly believes to have seduced his wife: 'The whirlpool!' Carnaby laments. 'It's got hold of *me*, and I'm going down, old man – and it looks black as hell.'

Each of these signature remarks gives the novel a terrific feeling of suppressed anxiety, the thought of people who fear the future, whose security is constantly imperilled, whose assumption that their comfortable existences are in danger is heightened by their inability to anticipate precisely what form the danger will take.

Part of this nervousness is simply a general presentiment of doom, the suspicion that life is changing for the worse, and at such a rapid rate that it is beyond the capacity of the average human being to resist it. As Rolfe puts it to Carnaby in one of their meditative conversations: 'There's something damnably wrong with us all – that's the one thing certain.' Another part is to do with an awareness of England's changing place in the world, and the call of an Imperial destiny – a subject which Gissing, as an arch-liberal and Kipling-mocker in the field of foreign policy, can be wonderfully ironic. But a third arises from the characters' sheer inanition. A few domestic servants excepted, nearly everyone in *The Whirlpool* is either a member of the leisured classes or clinging desperately to their subsidized fringes. The men, in particular, are uncomfortably aware of their superfluity, their fatal want of occupation, here in a world where women are beginning to claim a degree of social freedom that would have been unthought of half a century before. Several of the Rolfe–Carnaby dialogues turn ruefully on the fact of female liberty, and the danger that it may turn into licence

What follows, whether set in the West End concert halls or in the shadow of the Welsh mountains to which the Rolfes briefly decamp, is at one level a study in how people ought to behave, with a marked emphasis – Gissing being Gissing, with two unhappy marriages behind him and a desperate yearning for high-class female companionship – on how women ought to conduct themselves. Rolfe, a reformed rake in his late thirties – exactly Gissing's age when he came to write the book – is a confirmed bachelor, given to pious reflections on the disadvantages of the married state, and the particular misfortune of being attached to someone whose tastes and temperament you fail to share. At one point he muses on 'the supreme folly of hampering himself by marriage'; at another he formulates the general principle that it is 'an act of unaccountable folly to marry a woman from whom one differed on subjects that lay at the root of life'. Alma Frothingham, the woman who eventually breaks down this reserve, is the orphaned daughter of a financier driven to suicide; a statuesque girl with musical tastes and a hankering for fashionable life, whom Rolfe assumes, in one of those glacial judgements in which Gissing's fiction abounds, to have 'absorbed the vulgarity of her atmosphere'. Despite his good intentions, Rolfe is duly ensnared ('all his manhood was subdued and mocked by her scornful witchery') and the couple depart for North Wales, Rolfe assuming his wife's feigned enthusiasm for the simple life, living frugally and cultivating high ideals in close proximity to nature to be the real thing. Alma, alas, is not worth her husband's interest, neglects her children, the second of whom dies, admits to herself, if not to anyone else, that her desire to be a professional violinist stems from vanity rather than a love of music, and whose destructive effect on the people around her is compounded by jealousy. Carnaby's fatal assault on Cyrus Redgrave, the oily Croesus with whom Alma intrigues, takes place in the darkness of a suburban bungalow when, in a fit of passion, he mistakes Alma for his wife. Alma is only there because she suspects that Sybil Carnaby is bent on undermining Redgrave's support for her professional debut. Later, when she discovers that her husband is paying for the upkeep of two abandoned children, her first thought is that the boy and girl are products of a *mesalliance* that he is determined to keep quiet.

Meanwhile, the reader's opinion of Alma – never very high to start with – is being constantly recalibrated by wounding comparisons to the other women in whose orbit she moves: her stepmother Mrs Frothingham (conventionally minded but anxious to compensate those ruined by the bank smash out of her own resources); Sybil Carnaby (extravagant but, we infer, principled) and worthy Mrs Abbot (laid low by the financial crash but capable of finding new employment as a school-mistress). The most injurious contrast of all is with virtuous Mrs Morton, the wife of Rolfe's childhood friend, who lives modestly in the country, is meekness personified and devotes herself to housekeeping and her children. One forgives Gissing his bromides about Mrs Morton, her selfless devotion to hearth and home and the domestic idyll in which she and her husband calmly repose, in the knowledge that they are the result of a frustrated idealism. He would have liked nothing better than to live a reclusive life in a country town with a gentlewomanly helpmeet who was clever enough for him to talk to, rather than labour on in Epsom with the cantankerous and increasingly unstable Edith. That, in the end, none of these immensely pointed critiques turns Alma into a caricature is a tribute to the sureness of Gissing's psychological touch. The scenes in which she prepares for her professional unveiling, for example, or tries to impress a sympathetic Mrs Abbot with the range of her accomplishments have an objectivity, a sense of the kind of person Alma is, that some of her husband's assessments of his wife's character rather lack: restless, dissatisfied, always searching for an excitement that child-bearing and servant-handling will never provide, forever trying to shore up her personal mythology of artistry and moral scrupulousness. As it is, Alma betrays herself from one utterance to the next, but her awareness of the tricks she is playing, both on herself and the people around her, give her a complexity she would otherwise struggle to acquire. It is the same with her recourse – half careless, half grimly determined – to the 'fashionable narcotic' that will help her sleep, with consequences that the experienced reader of Victorian fiction can see coming half a dozen chapters off. Neither, strictly speaking, are the various catastrophes Alma provokes altogether her fault. A stronger-minded husband than Rolfe would have taken her in hand, curbed her impetuousness, taken her away from the London charivari of malign influences and fairweather friends.

If all this makes *The Whirlpool* sound like a case study in late nineteenth century environmentalism, then Gissing's insistence that we are conditioned by the company we keep is ultimately a false trail. More than one contemporary critic observed that his keenness on the debasing influence of milieu – as striking here as it is in his slum novels – is deceptive, for the relentlessness of his naturalism implies that most human beings will be unhappy wherever they live, and that the only solution to life's miseries is a resolute stoicism. Rolfe at one point argues that the best kind of education for Walter would be one 'which hardened his skin and blunted his sympathies... The thing is, to get through life with as little suffering as possible.' Just as one of the novel's satisfactions lies in its undeviating procedural line, so another rests in the knowledge of what awaited Gissing in the last six years of his life: a period in which failing health was to a certain extent compensated for by the attentions of Gabrielle Fleury, the intellectual companion whose vision he had pursued for most of his adult life. Written in the shadow of a disintegrating marriage, bitterly opposed to nearly everything that the late-Victorian age held dear, barely disguising a fatalism that is as much personal as philosophical, *The Whirlpool* is a convincing argument for Gissing's claim, quite as credible as Hardy's, to be regarded as the last great Victorian novelist.

Introduction to Penguin Modern Classics edition of The Whirlpool,
2015

UPWARDLY MOBILE: H.G. WELLS AND *KIPPS*

When John Updike criticised Kingsley Amis for what he called his 'fussy social judgments' he was making a complaint about the English novel that could have been filed at practically any time over the past two hundred years: the idea that, though a work of fiction may contain romance and even melodrama, though it may purport to bring vast acreages of our national life under a single, centralising lens, at its heart is likely to lie a kind of social primer, a style guide to behaviour in which most of the questions about how human beings should think and act are reduced to simple etiquette. To a certain kind of nineteenth-century critic, particularly one with an eye trained on the view beyond the study window, even the best mid-Victorian novel could quickly transform itself into a series of immensely exacting social protocols: it was Walter Bagehot who once suggested that Thackeray's animating force as a novelist was a determination to prove that ninth-rate people were actually tenth-rate.

No doubt Bagehot and Updike have a point – and one remembers the luckless Margaret Peel in *Lucky Jim*, damned for her over-bright make-up and arty skirts – and yet the 'society' in which most writers take some sort of interest is only the sum of its preoccupations: the novelist set down in it tends to write about its quirks in the same spirit of enquiry that Jack London brings to the fauna of the Yukon trail, and in the knowledge that a moral judgment based on the way in which a person raises a tea-cup is no less fascinating for being built on snobbery. Then there is the fact that most English novels about social advancement – most English novels, that is – have three distinct moral perspectives: the standpoint of the hero, making his or her ascent; the standpoint of the particular social group in which that ascent is being fashioned; and the standpoint of the writer himself. In a novel like *Kipps*, the contrasts are rendered all the sharper by the author's own social triumphs, his quarrel with both the part of society he came from and the part in which he ended up, and the by no means inconsiderable matter of his own personality.

The theme of *Kipps* (1905), Wells's second 'proper' novel after a high-octane grounding in scientific romance, would have been all-too familiar to the great Victorians from whom he took so much of his inspiration. Essentially its concerns are those of *Great Expectations* (1861) or an early Thackeray sketch such as 'Cox's Diary' (1840): what happens if you rescue someone from a comparatively low rung of society, give him a life-transforming sum of money and try to make a 'gentleman' out of him. But the difference between Artie Kipps and Thackeray's Barber Cox, whose tuft-hunting wife inherits a fortune and destroys her family's happiness into the bargain, is that Wells, having climbed up from society's lower rung himself, actively sympathises with his hero. He may mock Kipps's ambitions, he may insist that his aspirations are not worth the having, but in the end class solidarity always wins out, if only because Kipps is a backward projection of Wells himself, minus the genius – a harmless, averagely accomplished lower-middle-class boy, condemned to the drudging, joyless life of the shopkeeper's assistant until an unexpected legacy sets him free.

Orphaned and illegitimate, with a cloud of fog hanging over almost every aspect of his early life, Kipps is brought up in the sequestered Kentish town of New Romney by an aged uncle and aunt, has his intelligence systematically warped in a pretentious private school and is then apprenticed to a dim-witted but obstreperous Folkestone draper. His salvation lies in an unforeseen £26,000 – £2 million, say, at current values – left to him by his regretful grandfather. Predictably, Kipps's social rise begins from the moment he steps out of the lawyer's office (the scene in which he goes back to New Romney to break the news to his relatives is one of the funniest in the book) and before two months are up he is fearfully at large in Folkestone 'society', tremulously engaged to a 'lady', living in his grandfather's house and nervously acclimatising himself to a world of servants, dressing for dinner and genteel entertainment.

At the same time, Wells's 'message' is a comparatively subtle one. It is not just that social aspirations of any kind are faintly ridiculous, and that no one in their right mind would want to sacrifice the companionship of people of their own social class for dismal little dinners and mock-refined chatter about art. Rather, Wells insists, social distinctions are unavoidable because they exist in every section of society. The poorest street in Camberwell will be riven by class prejudice, this argument runs, because the dustman will always think himself superior to the rat-catcher next door. The old Kippses in their flyblown shop set the tone for their nephew's upbringing: 'They were always very suspicious about their neighbours and other people generally; they feared the 'low' and they hated and despised the 'stuck up' and so they 'kept themselves *to* themselves' according to the English ideal.' It is the same in Kipps's dreadful private school, most of whose inmates are sent there not for an education but to 'demonstrate the dignity of their parents and guardians', and possibly worse in Mr Sheldrake's draper's establishment, which is all sham-gentility and slave-driven shop-girls thanking God at that least they are a cut above skivvies.

Set against this backdrop of petty one-upmanship, in which everyone is either staring enviously at their 'betters' or looking down their noses at inferior competition stranded beneath the salt, Miss Walsingham, whom Kipps courts and is accepted by almost by accident, is a kind of molten goddess, as far removed from aitch-dropping Flo Bates from the cash desk as a duchess from a dairy maid, by whose conniving mother and swindling solicitor brother Kipps is completely bamboozled. And yet the circle in which Miss Walsingham moves, and on which, as an interesting specimen of shabby-genteel poverty, she quietly sponges, is simply an up-market version of the one Kipps has always known: 'There was the same subtle sense of social gradation that had moved Mrs Kipps to prohibit intercourse with labourers' children, and the same dread of anything 'common' that had kept the personal quality of Mr Shalford's establishment so high.' The only thing that has been detached from this landscape of gentrified party-going and butler-haunted vestibules, thanks to the £26,000, is the doubt over Kipps's admission ticket.

Meanwhile, as Kipps is inducted into the mysteries of 'calling', introduced to the local vicar, who is, extraordinarily, both the Reverend *and* Honourable, and given an all-purpose cultural education courtesy of his fast friend Mr Chester Coote, some other judgments are moving silently into view. These, significantly enough, are Wells's own. One of the most revealing passages involves an elaborate description of the study in which Mr Coote, a high-minded bachelor who lives with his 'artistic' spinster sinister, occupies his leisure hours: a little bedroom 'put to studious uses' and featuring 'an array of things he had been led to believe indicative of culture and refinement. These include reproductions of works by Rossetti and Watts. There is also a selection of books – 'no worse an array of books that you find in any public library,' Wells helpfully glosses – copies of the *Bookman*, a well-known middlebrow periodical of the day ('no English paper can have been more cosily, more lavishly, more exclusively devoted to the spirit of *belles-lettres*' John Gross once noted) and much sagacious advice from Mr Coote on 'the one serious book' a cultivated man ought to read each week.

This is Wells the switched-on metropolitan intellectual, the friend of Gissing and Henry James, having a little fun with a specimen of the faded provincial culture he had doubtless had many opportunities of observing in his youth, and as you might expect Mr Coote ('the exemplary Coote') is instantly derided as the kind of man who picks up a copy of *Sesame and Lilies* in the same spirit that he pulls on a pair of lavender gloves, someone to whom the whole idea of 'culture' is at best an accessory and at worst a means to an end. At the same time there is something faintly superfluous about this demolition, the sense of a character who is not being brought into a book for his own sake but to prove a point, as well as a suspicion that it would be perfectly possible to judge Wells himself by standards even more exacting than these and find him just as wanting as Mr Chester Coote.

In setting out the novel's denouement, Wells is true to his class: he has Kipps rebel, throw over his ladylike fiancée for Ann Pornick, the servant girl he loved as a child, and be swindled by Miss Walsingham's scapegrace brother. The moral of *Kipps*, then, is the moral of *Great Expectations* brought forward to the Edwardian age: don't throw over the class you were born into; don't imagine that the process of 'bettering yourself' won't involve huge amounts of moral compromise and self-delusion, or that your relationships with the people you knew in your previous life can persist unhindered – see, for instance, the very pointed scene in which Kipps, out listening to an open-air concert with his faithful attendant Mr Coote, comes across a couple of sarcastic cronies from the draper's shop. While there are times when Wells canvasses the relative merits of other modes of life – for example the mild bohemianism of Kipps's play-writing chum Chitterlow, and the socialism idiosyncratically preached by Sid Pornick's journalist lodger Masterman – the answer to the pressing question of what he actually wants from the world he surveys, and how he imagines its social arrangements might be improved, comes in an odd little passage towards the end.

The stimulus is a corking row between Kipps and Ann, in their newly-built house, after a disastrous visit by the family of the Rev. G. Porrett Smith who assume that Ann, fresh from enamelling the upstairs floor, is a servant. 'The stupid little tragedies of these clipped and limited lives' Wells laments, before going on to condemn 'the anti-soul… the ruling power of this land, Stupidity.' The Kippses, he decides, are merely children – 'children who feel pain, who are naughty and muddled and suffer, and do not understand why.' So what, in the last resort, does

Wells want? He wants a world in which people will behave better to each other, a world in which honest aspiration and fellow-feeling won't automatically be snuffed out by snobbery and hidebound tradition, a world in which 'equality' is not a dirty world – Kipps at one point declares himself a 'Socialist' after a humiliating stay at a classy London hotel – but it will also be a world in which people like H.G. Wells are allowed to luxuriate and prosper. On one level *Kipps* is an expose of an outdated social system, a life based fundamentally on the principle of fooling yourself, but is also, you imagine, an *apologia pro vita sua*.

What remains is a kind of sentimental realism, in which the happy ending altogether fails to disguise some of the genuine horrors that lurk behind the wainscoting of the average late-nineteenth century interior: the out-of-work drapers' assistants quietly starving to death in library reading rooms, tubercular journalists coughing their guts out in rented garrets. Wells was never a realist in the textbook sense of the word, and the brute matter-of-factness of a contemporary American naturalist like Dreiser or Upton Sinclair was denied him both by the tradition in which he wrote and, even more important, the view that he took of the world. In his famous essay 'Wells, Hitler and the World State' (1941), Orwell proposed that Wells was simply 'too sane' for the mid-twentieth landscape of marching armies and lofted flags. By the time of his death in 1946 he openly despaired at the state of the world he found himself in. Here in 1905 he was merely exasperated, confident that a little more collective action, a little more personal resonance, could change things for the better.

'I don't suppose there ever was a chap quite like me before' Kipps tells his wife on the novel's final page. In strict, taxonomic terms this is a red herring, for the English novel of the previous century is full of bewildered socio-economic migrants of the Kipps sort, ripe to be exploited by the unscrupulous predators of the gentlemanly drawing-room. On the other hand, no previous novelist had Wells's ability, borne of bitter, personal experience, to decode the assumptions on which a certain kind of lower-middle-class life was based. *Kipps*, consequently, is a number of things all at once – a disguised autobiography, an economic clarion call, a successful attempt to extend the English novel's social range, but it is, above all, a horribly funny book written by a man who still believed that the most effective way of attacking something was to laugh at it.

Introduction to Weidenfeld & Nicolson edition of Kipps, *2010*

WODEHOUSE'S GHOSTS: *PSMITH IN THE CITY*

Rupert, subsequently Ronald, Psmith – the 'P' silent as in physic, ptarmigan and psithisis – made his fictional debut in 'The Lost Lambs', a serial for the boys' magazine *The Captain*, in 1908 and the source of the novel *Mike and Psmith* (1909). There were later, more adult versions of Psmith – the New York magazine proprietor of *Psmith Journalist* (1915) and the masquerading poet of *Leave it to Psmith* (1923), but experienced Wodehouse-fanciers generally agree that his most spectacular flowering comes in *Psmith in the City*, as 'The New Fold' again written for *The Captain* between 1908 and 1909 and first published in volume form by A. & C. Black on 23 September 1910.

In later life Wodehouse was keen to play down Psmith's appeal. Questioned by a *Paris Review* interviewer not long before his death in 1975, he acknowledged that 'people sometimes want to know why I didn't go on with Psmith', while insisting that he 'didn't think the things that made him funny as a very young man would be funny in an older man.' Among the characteristics that Wodehouse professed to dislike was 'a very boring sort of way of expressing himself', in particular Psmith's habit of 'calling everybody comrade and that sort of thing. I couldn't go with him.'

In fact, this attempt to undermine Psmith's status in the Wodehouse pantheon is faintly disingenuous. As Robert McCrum shows in his excellent biography *Wodehouse: A Life* (2004), until at least the mid-1920s it was Psmith, far more than such later staples of the canon as Jeeves (first appearance 1916) or Lord Emsworth on whom his reputation depended. As late as 1936, for example, he could be found telling his friend Bill Townend, in relation to some future project, that 'Psmith is a major character... If I am going to have Psmith in a story he must be in the big situation.'

But what sort of a comic character is Psmith? Based, as Wodehouse later admitted, on his friend Rupert D'Oyly Carte, he is a kind of super-charged, upper-class version of the 'masher' or 'knut' of the Edwardian comic paper, the suave expositor of a style guide to which his debased provincial cousin. H. G. Wells's Arthur Kipps, with his vertiginous collars and his curly-brimmed hat, can only dowdily aspire. Tall, monocled, sauntering through London clubland in the 'faultless evening dress of which the female novelist is so fond', inexpressibly pained by solecisms of speech or dress ('Comrade Bannister has blown into the office today in patent leather boots with white kid uppers, as I believe the technical term is'), a repository for every choice expression known to the pre-Great War slang dictionary, Psmith is also a tough customer, a sharp operator, and most of the humour comes from the succession of adversaries – schoolmasters, bank managers, gangsters – who, whatever their claims to status and superiority, are simply not up to the Old Etonian's fighting weight. Even more significant, and another source of comic tension in a novel built on the public school codes of Wodehouse's days at Dulwich College, Psmith is, at heart, fundamentally immoral, never afraid to hit below the belt if the situation demands it and capable of breath-taking feats of subterfuge and duplicity.

In his essay 'In Defence of P.G. Wodehouse' (1945), written to rebut the allegations of treachery that followed Wodehouse's war-time broadcasts on Berlin radio, George Orwell described *Psmith in the City* as 'psychologically the most revealing book of Wodehouse's early period' (Orwell sent a copy to his first wife, Eileen as she lay in hospital awaiting the operation that would kill her: she reported that she 'laughed out loud.') The revelation lies in Wodehouse's trick of transferring his own late-teenage experiences as a bank-clerk to Mike Jackson, previously an ornament of the Wrykyn First XI, now set to work as an office boy at £54 a year. Like Mike, pitch-forked into the postal department of the 'New Asiatic Bank' by a financially embarrassed father who can no longer afford to send him to university, the 18 year-old Wodehouse had spent two years in the Lombard Street branch of the Hong Kong & Shanghai Bank – not a complete throwing over of family tradition (Wodehouse *pere* was an old colonial hand) but no kind of destiny to a boy who had set his heart on Oxford.

Although Wodehouse later claimed to have enjoyed his time in Lombard Street ('I liked the companionship – we had an awfully nice crowd') much of the novel burns with a wholly unmediated sense of personal hurt. The bank itself is a 'blighted institution'; the business transacted there is 'irksome' and the monotony 'appalling'. And this is not simply Wodehouse being funny: McCrum notes the profound sense of alienation that hangs over Mike's early days in the Square Mile, and there is a queer little passage towards the end of the book which imagines commercial life in straightforwardly mechanistic terms. 'After all, most people look on the cashier of a bank as a sort of human slot-machine. You put in your cheque, and out comes money. It is no affair of yours whether life is treating the machine well or ill that day.'

All this gives *Psmith in the City* a terrific air of authenticity. My father, who started working for the Norwich Union Insurance Company in the 1930s (and, incidentally, at a salary even feebler than Mike Jackson's) always maintained that it was the only novel that gave an accurate picture of what working in a office was like from the angle of the ground-down clerk: the protocols of arrival and departure, the pettifogging regulations, the routine subservience to tedious officialdom, above all the sense, common to a junior staff plucked from cricket fields and study-bedrooms, that the future has stopped being a roseate blur and become sharp, hard and tangible. A future, more to the point, in which any kind of rebellion is doomed to failure. As Mike puts it:

'What I mean to say is, it isn't like a school. If you wanted to score off a master at school, you could always rag and so on. But here you can't. How can you rag a man who's sitting all day in a room of his own, while you're sitting at a desk at the other end of the building?'

From the moment that Mike looks up from his letter-strewn desk to find his old school-chum (despatched to the bank on a parental whim) tapping him on the shoulder, *Psmith in the City* pursues a curious kind of double life: on the one hand a scrupulous piece of early twentieth-century social realism, in which a lonely and potentially mutinous adolescent is forced to get to grips with some of the realities of commerce; on the other, a glorious exercise in wish fulfilment in which the pair set about getting their own back on stately Mr Bickersdyke, the bank's exacting manager. In much the same way, when building up the novel's atmosphere, Wodehouse follows two distinct chronological lines. Some of the supporting detail, naturally, comes from his memories of labouring for the Hongkong & Shanghai in 1900–1902. Rather more, with an eye on the topicality demanded by readers of *The Captain*, is taken from the late Edwardian era when the novel was being written.

At one point, determined to conciliate the Manchester United-supporting Mr Rossiter, the postal department's somewhat iracible head, Psmith sets out to acquire a working knowledge of Association Football. 'By the end of the fortnight he knew what was the favourite breakfast-food of J. Turnbull; what Sandy Turnbull wore next to his skin; and who, in the opinion of Meredith, was England's leading politician.' These are Jimmy Turnbull, his celebrated namesake Sandy, scorer of the goal that saw off Bristol City in the 1909 F.A. Cup Final and the flying winger Billy Meredith, and their inclusion establishes the novel's absolute up-to-dateness in the minds of its first batch of readers. Jimmy Turnbull, for example, arrived at Old Trafford in 1907, while Sandy's *annus mirabilis* was the season 1907/8 in which his 25 goals helped the club secure the First Division championship.

The same attention to detail is shines off the repeated references to variety hall entertainers. At the political meeting at 'Kenningford', where Psmith goes to heckle Mr Bickersdyke, an aspiring Tory MP, the opening speaker is a Scots peer whose accent reminds the crowd of Harry Lauder ('They invited him to be a pal and sing 'The Saftest of the Family'. Or, failing that, 'I Love a Lassie.' Finding they could not induce him to do this, they did it themselves.') Lauder's signature tune, 'I Love a Lassie', was first aired in 1907. Again, the supporting detail comes not from the years in which Wodehouse laboured in Lombard Street but from the time in which he sat down to remember it.

Nowhere is the eye for minutiae, and for particular sub-strata of Edwardian bourgeois life, more marked than in the chapters that cover Mike and Psmith's dealings with the shy but amiable head cashier, Mr Waller. Unlike his erstwhile chum Bickersdyke, who has risen in the world and foresworn the radical opinions of his youth (information Psmith is pleased to secure) Mr Waller is a secret socialist. Persuaded by Psmith that he, too, is a worker in the cause ('Yours for the Revolution?') Waller invites the pair of them to hear him address the Sunday afternoon crowd at Clapham Common. The scenes that follow, both at this suburban version of Speaker's Corner and afterwards at supper *chez* Waller are sharply realised: not bringing the eye that a Wells, or, a little earlier, a Gissing would have brought to them, but leaving the reader in no doubt that at some point in his life Wodehouse had sat in something very like Mr Waller's frigid drawing-room with a keen anthropological interest.

A novel which features, among other things, a socialist harangue on Clapham Common and a bank manager's attempt to enter parliament might be expected to have some kind of political underpinning. But *Psmith in the City*'s 'politics', such as they are, turn out to be only a kind of Conservatism by default. At one level, all political activity, whether Mr Waller's savage oratory ('Well, I am perhaps a little bitter… A little mordant and ironical') or Mr Bickersdyke's pompous lectures to his constituents, is simply grist to Wodehouse's mill. At another, however unobtrusively, vested interests are undeniably at stake. Wodehouse, for example, has the proper *rentier* attitude to the rowdier element among the free and independent electors of 'Kenningford' (which looks like an amalgam of Kennington and Deptford): 'These looked on elections as Heaven-sent opportunities for making a great deal of noise. They attended meetings to extract amusement from them; and they voted, when they voted, quite irresponsibly.'

Again, when Mr Bickersdyke, slyly interrupted by Psmith, falters in his speech, Wodehouse notes that he had 'lost his audience. A moment before he had grasped them and played on their minds (or what passed for minds down in Kenningford) as on a stringed instrument.' Psmith, too, is at his most unaffectedly snobbish when *en route* to Mr Waller's Sunday entertainment ('The first thing to do is to ascertain that such a place as Clapham Common really exists') and, arguably, worse on the journey back ('Do you realise, Comrade Jackson, the thing that has happened? I am riding on a tram. I, Psmith, have paid a penny for a ticket on a tram.' What undermines this, and to a certain extent redeems it, is the public school insistence on 'fair play'. Listening to the head cashier speak, Mike is outraged by the jeering of the crowd and, when the Edwardian equivalent of a hoodie throws a stone, wades in on his boss's behalf and is narrowly rescued from a baying mob. In a similar act of quixotry, Mike opts to carry the can when Mr Waller is threatened with the sack for cashing a forged cheque.

It is not true, on the other hand, to say that Wodehouse has no political awareness at all, for a part of him sees very clearly the kind of low-level corruption and petty conspiring on which so much of Edwardian life is based. There is a rather significant scene, for instance, in which Psmith, having sprung Mike from the mob and onto the waiting tram, matter-of-factly bribes both the conductor and an investigating policeman to silence. To Wodehouse this seems the most natural thing in the world, as well as an excuse for comic remarks about 'the slight softening of the frigidity of the constable's manner.' The scene's wider implication – why is it that a couple of well-bred young men should be able to evade a police enquiry simply because they have money? – hardly occurs to Wodehouse, or, if it does, only as a source of humour. It is the same with Mr Bickersdyke and his ambitions. The idea that the capitalist banking system is a sort of licensed swindle, predicated on the willingness of thousands of worker drones to be exploited never strays across Mike's mind. If pressed, he would probably say that bank managers should be just a little less Olympian, a little less vindictive, or – Mr Bickersdyke's particular crime in the novel's opening pages – a little less prone to walk behind the bowler's arm when the batsman is two runs short of his century.

What allows Wodehouse to get away with these evasions, it might be argued, is that his comedy is essentially a matter of technique, practically an exercise in pure form, like a clerihew or a Lear limerick. The jokes may rely on questions of status or self-aggrandisement, but at their core generally lies only an extravagant delight in repartee, in language used for no other purpose than to demonstrate the kind of effects of which language is capable. Possibly the funniest line in the novel comes when Mr Bickersdyke upbraids Psmith for spending his evenings haunting the corridors of the 'Senior Conservative Club' where the bank manager goes to dine and play bridge. 'I can only assume that you are not in your right mind' Mr Bickersdyke deposes. 'You follow me about in my club.' 'Our club, sir' Psmith murmurs in response. Or there is the pacification of Mr Rossiter, by way of feigned enthusiasm for Turnbull J. and S., and Billy Meredith: 'By kindness… By tact and kindness. That is how it is done. I do not despair of training Comrade Rossiter one of these days to jump through paper hoops.'

Psmith in the City ends back in fantasy land, with Mr

Bickersdyke effectively blackmailed by Psmith's acquisition of the record of the 'Tulse Hill Parliament', scene of his youthful indiscretions, Mike summoned to play cricket for his county at Lords (where he scores a century) and Psmith senior consenting not only to send his son to Cambridge but to take Mike on board as a kind of up-market factotum. Looking at Psmith's later incarnations, one sees Wodehouse's point about the difficulty of transporting him beyond Edwardian late-teendom. The detail in *Psmith Journalist* is taken not from personal experience but from New York newspaper cuttings. *Leave it to Psmith* is a country house novel in which Mike turns out to be married and Psmith about to follow him down the same implausible primrose path. Only as schoolboys, or as apprentice bank-clerks, does Wodehouse really feel comfortable with them or have enough of an emotional connection with their predicaments to make their adventures convincing.

Wodehouse's great achievement in *Psmith in the City* was to harmonise the two sides of his early creative temperament – the wish-fulfilment side and the one rooted in bitter, personal experience – in a way that allows the comedy to exist alongside a species of realism that is otherwise largely absent from his work. Behind its jokes and its closing of its ranks against the aitch-dropper and the patent boot-wearer can be glimpsed the materials for a different kind of book – more downbeat, less supremely confident of the ability of fresh-faced public schoolboys to carry all before them, haunted by the ghosts of Bennett and Wells. Of all Wodehouse's novels it is the one in which he can be detected writing against the grain of his nature, with all the incidental friction that such exercises imply.

Times Literary Supplement, 2010

II. FICTION

MARY GAITSKILL'S LIBERAL GUILT

The Mare

No one could ever accuse Mary Gaitskill of casting her wares profligately before the public. Her far from compendious *oeuvre* extends to half-a-dozen books in a shade under three decades, and *The Mare* is only her third novel in a quarter of a century. Worse, the gaps between publication are getting longer: an abyss that may, in some degree, be down to *The Mare*'s prodigious length – in Gaitskill terms, that is. One had thought her an anorexic miniaturist, and now she bounces back with a 400-plus page epic on the very un-Gaitskill-like subject of a girl who learns to ride a horse.

The point is worth labouring, as Gaitskill's early short story collections – *Bad Behavior* (1988) and the superlative *Because They Wanted To* (1997) – were distinguished by some almost classically seedy casts and milieux. Their characters tended to be soured and vengeful screenwriters or no-hope girls fetched up perilously in the big city, and the great majority of them were there, or so the reader inferred, simply for Gaitskill to amuse herself with. The really striking aspect of both collections, it might be argued, is the author's cat-and-mouse treatment of the people she creates, where freedom is granted and then taken away in a paragraph's worth of banter.

Because They Wanted To, for example, skids to a halt with four linked stories assembled under what proves to be the deeply ambiguous heading 'The Wrong Thing.' Their narrator-heroine is a late-thirtysomething academic, who seeks relief from a succession of sedative heterosexual dates in a relationship with a younger woman named Erin. Erin, it turns out, is the kind of girl who enjoys being beaten by her lovers for the opportunity it allows her to connect with 'some deep mom pain.' Ingenuous and gauche, she is also tough and exacting, trifling (possibly) but not to be trifled with, and you sense not only that Gaitskill can't make up her mind about her, but that the consequent tension is what gives the piece – and the relationship – its bite. Futile or passionate? Life-affirming or merely desperate? You never quite know, and certainty would dull the effect.

The Mare is not like this at all. So much is it not like this at all, or, if so, only obliquely – more about this later – that experienced Gaitskill-fanciers may wonder if, all unknowing, they have suddenly been ushered into the presence of that notorious US book-trade artefact, the 'break-out novel', in which a formerly low-selling critic's darling grits his, or her, teeth and makes an unhesitating dash for the finishing tape of commercial success. In a recent *Bookseller* interview Gaitskill remarked that she had been counselled to try the 'young adult' market and declined the advice, but what remains can sometimes bear an odd resemblance to a pony club classic with a fair amount of salty dialogue and under-age sex dumped incongruously in its margins.

Velvet – short for 'Velveteen' – Vargas is a 12 year-old migrant from the Dominican Republic living in urban squalor with her furious mother Silvia and sarky younger sibling Dante. An epigraph advertises her link to Enid Bagnold's *National Velvet* (1944), later a vehicle for the young Elizabeth Taylor. Despatched to upstate New York by the 'Fresh Air Fund' (a philanthropic scheme for which Gaitskill has worked and to whom she pays tribute), she falls in with a welcoming middle-aged couple named Ginger and Paul. Although Paul, an academic, has a daughter from a previous marriage, his second wife – an ex-alcoholic avant-garde artist – is childless. She is also, as some early reflections on the fund's brochure reveal – this shows white children and black children holding flowers and smiling ('It was sentimental and flattering to white vanity and manipulative as hell. It was also irresistible') – a sucker for liberal guilt.

An early sign of the agenda Ginger imports to her surrogate parenting comes in her choice of suitable DVDs for Velvet to watch of an evening. Inexplicably, a promising discovery about a Hispanic girl 'who learns how to box and triumphs over her crappy life' gets a thumbs down. So does *Bend It Like Beckham*. Velvet is much happier with a film about a girl who discovers she is a princess. She also likes being read to from *The Lion, The Witch and the Wardrobe*, but disdains Ginger's experiments in abstract art ('Sometimes they weren't even shapes, they just looked like things you'd do in preschool.') Ginger, blithely assumes that her guest's presence 'made everything special' and that 'it was like we were both living a dream we had known from television and advertisements and children's books.'

One key theme here, naturally enough, is reliability. Ginger, who starts to take an interest in Velvet's misleading accounts of her schoolwork, is warned by a suspicious class teacher that 'This is a very manipulative kid.' On the other hand, neither she nor Paul are owning up to everything. A four-way narration (with one brief intervention from horse-trainer Beverly) involving husband, wife, Velvet and her mother – somewhat implausibly, as Silvia speaks only Spanish – weaves in and out of the various traumas with which everyone is afflicted to cover Velvet's chaotic home life, the badass girls at school and the no-good boys already molesting her at street-corners, Paul's affair with a student, Ginger's hook-up with a wrecked ex-boyfriend and her constant brooding over the death of her biker chick sister Melinda.

Meanwhile Velvet, a certain amount of girl-on-girl back-stabbing aside, has made a hit at the local stables, where she is adjudged a 'natural', establishes a bond with the usual untameable horse ('Fugly Girl', whom she rechristens 'Fiery Girl') is admonished for sass and a bad attitude but impresses the owner sufficiently to be chosen to compete in a gymkhana. These triumphs are enough to inspire Ginger with a hope that the whole Vargas family might like to relocate to Dutchess County, despite her inability to offer Silvia such basic information as the price of a carton of milk. Impressed by Ginger's fervour and flattered by his daughter Edie's assurance that she is 'so glad he is doing this', Paul is still sceptical to the point of informing his wife 'If you want to get hurt, use a grown-up, not a little girl.'

If *The Mare* is, at one level, a pointed little fable about power and manipulation, then it also has some harsh things to say about the Disneyfication of America. Beverly, the hard-as-nails subjugator of equine spirit notes that 'Even her, the tough black girl from the city… even she's been ruined by the Disneyfied horse-snot they sell in the multiplex.' But Ginger, in one of her shrewder moments, is smart enough to deduce that Disney idealism is about all that her protégé has in her locker. Romanticism, on this reading, is naturalism's partner-in-crime, and Velvet, when first cross-questioned about how she does in school, is careful to mark her 1s and 2s up to 3s and 4s – not because she wants to lie, Ginger reckons, but because she wants 'to create an ideal picture for me.'

None of this, it has to be said, has much to do with the materials in which Gaitskill used previously to deal. On the other hand it would be perfectly possible to argue that the qualities which distinguished *Because They Wanted To* – sarcasm, irony, the constant interrogation of motive, the procedural ambiguity – are still making their presence felt 20 years later, only in a slightly less conspicuous way. There is a revealing scene towards the end, when, waiting for the Vargas family to arrive at the gymkhana – you can guess the result – Paul reflects that 'there was something indescribably moving and dignified in the taxi's slow approach up the winding dirt road.' It is impossible to take this seriously, or rather to think that Gaitskill, on past evidence of her asperity, would ever take seriously a character who really thought this.

The same pungent scent of half-buried motive turns up in Ginger's monitoring of a couple of women who provide microphone commentary at the event, one of whom is thought to have 'the discordant profile of a drunk, deranged elf.' This is not mild, right-thinking Ginger speaking, but Gaitskill herself letting rip in the manner of her early stories. Not that she isn't also prepared to undermine Ginger by way of some nicely-judged pathetic fallacy vapidity, as when, at a Williamsburg party, she remarks that 'a gang of children ran round us like happy water.' Once again, however unobtrusively, Gaitskill is playing with her characters, giving them enough rope to hang themselves and then tugging it back just as the noose is about to tighten.

Direct and oddly oblique, simultaneously in your face and on the point of disappearing from view, *The Mare*'s ultimate effect hangs slightly out of reach. If it is an expose of white American liberal guilt, then a great deal of interior evidence suggests that it is a kind of skit on that guilt as well. Certainly, large parts of it cry out not to be taken at face value. To go back to that monumental early work, the people and their motives may have changed, but the gaze – wry, rueful, sometimes charitable, sometimes disgusted – remains the same.

Times Literary Supplement, 2016

GRANT RISK HALLBERG – *City on Fire*

Of all the countless allusions, ellipses and assorted little ironies in which *City of Fire* abounds, none is more incriminating than a passage on page 559 in which the splendidly named artist William Hamilton-Sweeney III, one of several possible heroes, sets about preparing a canvas in his dilapidated Bronx studio. The work is difficult and time-consuming, the tool-box hard to find and the physical labour involved unwelcome, but eventually William has the materials to nail together a wooden frame all of sixteen feet square. Why the prodigious size? Well, this is, apparently, 'a vestigial reflex' borne of an instinctive psycho-geographical twitch: '...blame New York', the paragraph goes on – and this is a work unusually keen on the wayside homily – 'he still had the conviction that American art should be Big.'

Several factors conspire to turn Grant Risk Hallberg's debut novel into a quintessentially American artefact. Most obviously there is its elephantine, inordinate and at times downright gratuitous length, the 300,000 or so words eventually served up putting it straight into the Dos Passos class of over-egged super-abundance. Then there are the millions of dollars already laid out on pre-publication advances and film-script parlayings. To this can be added the terrific self-consciousness with which the author sets out about his task, a determination to make every sentence-cluster add up to ten that would have been sufficient, in an earlier age, to inspire a genre painting entitled 'Hallberg writes the Great American Novel.' Finally, there is the fact that it takes place in that repository of stateside aspiration, the city – in this case the winded, cash-strapped and potentially explosive mid- to late '70s New York.

The first clutch of great American urban novels, by, among others, Theodore Dreiser, Upton Sinclair and James T. Farrell, were written upwards of 80 years ago – in the case of Dreiser's *Sister Carrie* as far back as 1900. For all the plenitude of their casts, and the sense of locales that can barely be pinned down, so rapidly are they expanding, their subject tends to be loneliness. Most of their characters are deracinated, solitary wanderers adrift on the tide, and nearly all of them harbour passages in which the ground-down hero prowls wretchedly through a forbidding cityscape whose sheer immensity is enough to remind him of his insignificance, his inability to fit it, to make the extraordinary structures and social arrangements surging up around him work to his advantage. *City on Fire* has exactly such a passage, in which Charlie, a drugged-up, strung-out and love-sick New York teen, steps out of doors:

> Underdressed, because in muzzy post-sleep he'd mistaken the brightness outside the basement for warmth… he jammed his fists in the pockets of his coat and did his best to lose himself in the empty sidestreets. It was impossible, of course; they were a perfect grid. He passed the ballfield, where he'd played pee-wee league, co-sponsored by the Jaycees or Kiwanis or something. When the wind kicked up, the loose cord from the yardarm made a racket against the flagless metal flagpole, an alarm that made his heart tense up like something was about to happen. Which was ridiculous, because whatever happened on Long Island, except people being born and people dying?

Mutatis mutandis, this could be *Sister Carrie*'s Hurstwood, his prospects shattered and his mistress about to decamp, tramping north along Seventh Avenue, 'idly fixing upon the Harlem river as an objective point' and then coming home to find her gone, or even Farrell's Studs Lonigan out looking for work in Depression-era Chicago with the future closing in on him like a giant pincer.

If the city, to Charlie, is less immediately threatening – unlike Studs and Hurstwood he will, at least, not end up dead – then there is still a powerful sense of *anomie* for which the eerie, densely itemised backdrop is partly responsible, especially as coming back across the dead grass of the baseball field he divines that 'someone was watching from one of the dug-outs.' People are always watching on Planet Hallberg– watching themselves reflected in mirrors, watching, with self-protecting vigilance, the people with whom family ties, relationships or happenstance force themselves to associate, watching the crowds that seethe around them and the stalkers, spies and eavesdroppers caballing at their core.

The first batch of American urban classics tended to be scrupulous works of naturalism, in which the representatives of puny mankind are eventually swept away by unappeasable natural forces. Studs Lonigan dies of pneumonia, with his fiancée pregnant and his father's bank foreclosing. *City on Fire*, alternatively, hangs – more or less – on a single, transgressive event: an attack in Grand Central Park on the snowy New Year's Eve of 1976 on a teenage girl named Samantha 'Sam' Ciccario. Though beaten into a coma, Sam survives, the 'convergence of a thousand thousand stories' a journalist involved in the case reflects, to the shadow of whose 'glass-coffined beauty' every other character in the novel is inexorably drawn.

In work of 900-plus pages there are, inevitably, quite a lot of these. They include Charlie, her sort-of aspiring boyfriend who arrives at the crime scene a moment or two late and then guiltily skedaddles, Mercer Goodman, a Dixie-born black schoolteacher, potential novelist and boyfriend to heroin-addled, trustafarian William, and sturdy Keith Lamplighter (alert readers will already have spotted the figurative import of some of Hallberg's surnames), Sam's secret but now ex-lover, whose wife Regan is William's sister and PR frontwoman for the family finance house. Also periodically on call are Richard Groskoph, a veteran journalist initially writing a piece about Sam's firework-manufacturing father Carmine, his neighbour Jenny Nguyen, who just happens to work for William's art-dealing chum Bruno, Pulaski, the about-to-retire detective assigned to the case, and the members of an anarchist commune called the Post-Humanists (these have names like Sewer Girl and Nicky Chaos) connected to a now defunct punk band named Ex Post Facto for whom William, under the alias of 'Billy Three-Sticks', once sang lead.

Here in the history of New York's Bicentennial Year alternative music scene lies the novel's atmospheric backdrop, the framework for an endless series of patiently quarried references to Patti Smith's *Horses*, Television's *Marquee Moon* and couture strategies that will 'make the jeans look tighter' as if their wearer were 'the fifth Ramone', faltering only in its introduction of Sid Vicious's name some months before this legendary punk icon rose from obscurity to a role as the Sex Pistols' bass player. Running alongside, on the other hand, is a more conventional grounding in financial chicanery, blackmail and manipulation, centred on the deeply sinister figure of Amory Gould, the brother of William and Regan's step-mother. As the casualty count rises, and Mercer and Jenny find themselves alerting the authorities to the clues contained in Sam's self-penned fanzine, it is to the white-haired' demon uncle that all plot lines irrevocably return.

Meanwhile, there is another character lurking in the background. This is New York itself, so constantly anthropomorphised that its interventions in the text come round as regularly as evidence of Amory's wheeler-dealing, or the Post-Humanists' pilfered firework-powder bomb plot that introduces the novel's finale. Mercer, dragged by William into a doorway clinch, understands that this is why 'the city had summoned him.' On another occasion, watching the street life ebb and flow around him, he – somewhat stagily – divines that 'this was what the city bestowed that novels couldn't: not what you needed in order to live, but what made the living worth doing in the first place.' As well as turning people crazy, and dying on its feet, New York is also figuratively conjoined with the graveyard of St Mark's in-the-Bowery, where Pulaski at one point fetches up, 'a city where we'd all dwell.'

If these iterations eventually become rather quaint, then they also serve to underline *City on Fire*'s chronological grounding. For this, written by a 35 year-old, born half-a-decade after the Ramones' first album broke upon the record racks, is transparently an historical novel, whose elaborate garnishes on such subjects as firework manufacture or the great power shut-down of July 1977 that dominates the final chapters are a product of research rather than memory. The significance of this chronicler's approach becomes even more important about half-way through when Hallberg starts to sketch in his characters' back stories – Regan's secret abortion, Keith's induction into the firm – his point being that no record of the clamorous and morally exhausted American Seventies can ignore the decade that went before.

It also helps to explain Hallberg's attitude to his allusions, courteous to a fault in not advertising to readers things they may already know. There is no need to identify 'the fat guy on *Saturday Night Live*' as John Belushi: you either score this point or lose it. On the other hand, you get the feeling that the phrase about 'tuxed fucks' at a party – straight out of Martin Amis's *Money* – is just a happy accident. *City of Fire* turns out to be full of happy accidents and also a fair amount of sleight-of-hand. The prose style alternates between the convincing flourish (a curtain rippling 'as from the swift, soft movements of mice') and the over-emphatic, as when Keith and Regan, their marriage in tatters, stand facing each other, 'her arms crossed, his hanging like butchered meat at his sides.' In the end, though, the novel's excessive length is its undoing: characters flee to the margins to be half-forgotten before they shakily re-emerge; emotional touch-paper gets damped down by the steady drip of detail. For all the vigour of its engagement, and its cast of intent, solitary wanderers, the result is, rather like William's gargantuan picture frame, sometimes paralysed by the sheer weight of its ambition.

Times Literary Supplement, 2015

RUSHDIE'S TRUMP CARD

SALMAN RUSHDIE – *The Golden House*

To New York, in the opening days of the Obama presidency, from the country which for some reason cannot be named but is in fact India, in conditions of considerable secrecy, come the Golden clan. Their number is initially set at four: ageing but sappy potentate Nero ('he exuded a heavy, cheap odour, the unmistakable smell of crass, despotic danger'); stolid eldest son Petronius ('Petra'); sibling Apuleius ('Apu'); and a much younger half-brother, product of an indiscreet liaison with a woman who can't be named either, Dionysius ('D'). The original Mrs Golden is dead in the Mumbai terrorist outrage of 2008 and the classical re-imaginings are gamely kept up to the point where Nero can sometimes be found serenading himself with an antique violin.

Over the Goldens, who immediately establish themselves in a plush Manhattan mansion, hang well-nigh fathomless clouds of mystery. To Nero's no doubt shady past and the no doubt even shadier nature of his income can be added drink-sodden agoraphobic Petra's near-permanent sequestration in the bedroom where he sits devising computer games, Apu's newfound status as a radical artist and Occupy Movement hanger-on and Lower East Side girls' club volunteer and gender-conflicted D's struggles with his sexuality. Enigma number five swiftly declares itself in the form of flint-eyed Russian uber-babe Vasilia, unexpectedly promoted from mistress to wife on the strength of her command of 'a wordless language only men can understand.'

All this is punctiliously observed by Nero's much younger friend René, an aspiring film-maker who lives nearby with his elderly Belgian parents. It would be wrong to mark him down as

The Golden House's *raissoneur* in the strict, Somerset Maugham sense of the term, one who sits demurely on the half-way line commenting and analysing as the game whizzes by, for the longer the novel goes on the greater is his imbrication in it. René, sounding board, drinking chum and late-night confidante, is up to the neck in the Goldens' affairs, and never more so than when Vasilia, having got round a pre-nup agreement that there shall be no offspring, but alarmed by her husband's inability to clinch the deal, presses him into service ('I can be a little bit of a naughty girl' she confides) as the hands-on sperm donor.

It will scarcely need saying by this point – no more than a quarter of the way through a very long novel – that René's interest in the Goldens is professional as much as personal ('these were people worth spying on' he reflects) and that the life of the big house is being continuously cannibalised into a screenplay. For here we are, once again, in Rushdie-land, a world that has been periodically opening its doors to the impressionable reader since *Midnight's Children* scooped the Booker Prize all of 36 years ago – even longer if you count *Grimus*, an apprentice effort from 1975 – that brightly burnished fakir's bazaar where stories run riot on all sides, where horizon-hugging baroque alternates with finicking close-up rococo and where the grandeur of the concept is very often compromised by a sense of the effort put into its orchestration.

In this, our man's fourteenth piece of fiction, the reader's appreciation of all that inimitable Rushdie-semaphore, waving across from the Manhattan loft spaces and butler-haunted private gardens that are his current coign of vantage, will doubtless be sharpened by the thought that there is a second narrative going on here, booked to take in the parlous state of modern America. And so the Goldens' much-heralded decline, the old man's incremental crack-up, the three urns of funeral ash that accumulate on his desk top, the birth of the infant Vespasian and the disquieting news from back home alternate with bleak intimations of a nation given over to 'bitterly contested realities' and the rise of a 2016 presidential candidate known as 'the Joker', whose lies and evasions the propaganda films of René's girlfriend Suchitra aim to expose.

The odd thing about these constant attacks on the Tea Party, shock-jocks, alternative facts, 'phoniness, garishness, bigotry, vulgarity, violence, paranoia' and all the rest of it, is how unmediated they seem, and how extraneous to the main show, a case of Rushdie grafting his irritation with the Donald and all the smaller fry that sizzle in his slipstream onto an edifice that, despite one or two parallels with Nero's Mumbai, would probably survive without it. I was particularly struck, for example, by a page or so (some of the digressions really do digress) about the tendency to blame 'elites' for the world's current problems, not because the sentiments expressed are at all original, but because something horribly like them appears in Hanif Kureishi's recent novel, *The Nothing*.

Meanwhile, as the Goldens' past catches up with them and the last desperate strains of Nero's 1745 Guadagnini can be heard over the burning rooftops – there's an unexpected happy ending for René and son – the novel's real merits lie elsewhere. Rushdie is, as ever, excellent in conveying bitter, personal anger (as in the scene where René tries to come to grips with his parents' unnecessary death), while the stealthily hilarious (and potentially tragic) episode in which 'D' discusses his gender difficulties with a therapist offers a hint of what he could have done to Trump with a scalpel rather than carving him up with a chopper. You can't help thinking that the most effective books about the Trump presidency will be written long years from now, be set miles away from New York and not so much as refer to him either by name or alias.

Literary Review, 2017

CHILDREN BURNED AND CHILDREN BARTERED

TREZZA AZZOPARDI – *The Hiding Place*

Almost from the moment that it crash-landed onto the newspaper books pages in the summer of 2000, pundits have been worrying themselves over the precise genre category in which Trezza Azzopardi's first novel might be thought to repose. Noting the ground-down backdrop supplied by Cardiff's Tiger Bay district and the incidental references to the Dowlais ironworks and Penderyn, one or two critics went so far as to diagnose a 'Welsh novel'. To others, the presence of an ethnic sub-group rarely let loose in British fiction beyond the pages of a Soho crime caper, was proof of its status as a 'Maltese novel.' And yet a trawl through Azzopardi's later output – *Remember Me* (2004), *Winterton Blue* (2007) and *The Song House* (2010) – insists that this is a not a book about locale, or nationhood or psycho-geography, but the inaugural treatment of a set of themes that would go on to resonate through her work. These, it might be argued, are such tantalising abstracts as fear, subterfuge, buried memory and, above all, the constraints and concealments of family life.

The family on ramshackle display in *The Hiding Place* are the Gaucis, their number initially set at eight but diminishing almost from one chapter to the next. Of the six daughters, Marina is fostered out in highly suspicious circumstances to the family of a Maltese gangster with whom both her parents are dangerously embroiled, while pyromaniac Fran is eventually despatched to a children's home by the social services. Meanwhile betting-shop fixture Frankie, who first arrived in South Wales on the boat from Valetta in 1948, is preparing to desert his effervescing brood for a softer life back home. With or without him, the Gauci children are permanently stretched to breaking point, their dreams always liable to vanish into the ether when dad backs another loser, their accommodation forfeit to gambling losses, their mother Mary steadily less able to cope, individual and collective life forever swept up in an atmosphere of anger, debt, dereliction and the search for scapegoats.

'What really went on there... we only have this excerpt' Mark E. Smith intones at the beginning of The Fall classic 'Cruisers' Creek.' The buried and endlessly contested memory that lies at the heart of *The Hiding Place* has the same fragmentary quality – the terrifying sense that the tapestry of past life can never be properly stitched together as the vast majority of the pieces are so much unreconstitutable thread . Part of this, naturally, is to do with the novel's tripartite time-scale. Most of the action, the majority of it seen through the eyes of the youngest daughter Dolores ('Dol'), takes place in around 1965, but there are bleak look-backs to the calamitous accident that robbed cradle-bound Dol (born in 1960) of most of her left hand, while a 50 page coda finds the sisters reconvening at the family home long years later after their more or less abandoned mother's death.

All this gives the data offered to us early on in the book an oddly provisional quality, while establishing some of the questions it throws up in uncomfortably sharp relief. These involve such fundamental issues as Marina's parentage, Frankie's volcanic temperament – the birth of a sixth daughter is such an emotional blow that at first no one dares tell him the child is a girl – Mary's extra-curricular activities, the source of the money under the teapot and the headlong plunge of Salvatore, Frankie's erstwhile business partner, into the suffocating mud of Cardiff docks. If the reader has a fair idea of outcomes and motivation, then the truth nearly always seems ready to slip between the novel's cracks at a moment's notice.

'Children burnt and children bartered' Dol reflects at an early stage in the proceedings. 'Someone must be to blame.' While, on the one hand, *The Hiding Place* is a study of abuse, duplicity and straightforward lack of information – what really circumscribes the junior Gaucis' lives, we soon deduce, is how little they know about the forces that control them – then, on the other, it is a precise recreation of an historical environment, in this case the dense, incestuous stamping-ground of the South Wales Maltese, a community that gets by on bar-owning ('There are eighteen cafes on Bute Street' Dol reflects, 'and my father doesn't own any of them'), restaurant-provisioning and, we are led to infer, procuring. But this is the Swinging Sixties, a thousand miles away from home, and so the mantilla-draped shrines to the departed and the ceremonious rituals of birth, death and marriage march hand in hand with the latest news from Carnaby Street and the well-nigh forensic account of Celesta, Dols' elder sister, dressed up to the nines for a date in 'a two-piece of shocking crimplene pink, a turtle-neck blouse, and a pair of white patent lace-up boots which don't quite reach the knee.'

Significantly, the description of Celesta arrayed in her finery ('American Tan tights. A look of cool defiance on her face.') precedes a series of exchanges in which Mary's friend Eva tries to establish exactly which contemporary style icon is being patiently re-imagined here on the Gaucis' hearthrug beneath the layers of Mary Quant Matte and the new-moon curls. 'You're the image of Cilla' Eva first declares before abruptly changing tack to assure her that 'No, I tell a lie, it's Dusty.' It turns out that Celesta has her sights neither on Cilla Black nor Dusty Springfield but the fringe popularised by *Ready Steady Go*'s pop picker Cathy McGowan ('I'll give it five.') But the symbolism of these passages carries them far beyond Azzopardi's need to tether her characters in a recognisable pop-cultural milieu. Not only is the scene between teenage girl and maternal sidekick enacted in a room containing two photographs of Celesta as a small child in a bridesmaid's dress ('My father loves this picture') and clutching a Communion Book, but it ends with her softly drawing the powder-puff across her younger sister's cheek to erase a temporary scar. Taking her cue, Dol 'holds out my bad hand for mending.'

The Hiding Place is full of eerie little symbolic episodes of this kind. One or two of them are bound up in the popular music of the day, which flows across the claustrophobic interiors in which the novel is set in an uncontrollable torrent and encourages the characters to reckon up their destinies while listening to Julie London's 'Cry Me a River' or carolling Cliff Richard's 'Living Doll', a song which Dol understandably assumes 'is about me.' Far more, though, are to do with flesh, whether living or dead, and its niggling connections to the air of existential dread that hangs over their attempts to chart a passage through life. Some of this metaphorical gesturing is relatively unobtrusive, as in Celesta's job at the Co-op meat counter, from which she returns bearing packets of Bowyer's Pork Sausages and parcels of bacon (her father wolfs these down raw) and tempting invitations from her love-smitten manager, Markus. It takes a while for the reader to establish that Celesta is effectively a piece of meat herself – a twitch at the elbow that becomes an emphatic tug once her Frankie schemes to marry her off to a middle-aged widower.

To balance this stealthy emblem-mongering are a handful of flaring moments in which Azzopardi's figurative sub-text becomes abundantly clear. One might note the awful, illusion-shattering morning of Celesta's marriage when Dol catches her father in the act of dismembering a pet rabbit, gleefully ripping out the animal's heart with his fingers for use in a wedding dish. Or there is the scene a page or two before in which Salvatore, proudly inspecting the nuptial baked meats locked up in his outhouse, catches sight of a rat nibbling at one of the pie-crusts, whacks it with a spade and looks on, aghast, as a hock of ham flies up at him 'like a severed limb' before bouncing away onto the flagstones. Worst of all, perhaps, is another rabbit episode in which the infant Dol tampers with a newly-born litter left out in the back-yard pen, causing the mother to devour its young, and is told that this is the result of her 'interfering.' Clearly, there are other things being interfered with here, if not metaphorically eaten alive, way beyond the confines of the rabbit hutch.

And so Azzopardi's title turns out to be a well-disguised play on words. The Gaucis' backstreet tenement may be a place where you can try to conceal yourself from the deeply demoralising forces marshalled against you, but it is also a place in which secrets are hidden, defying the attempts of Dol and her sisters to winkle them out and make sense of their implications. Inevitably, these silences and evasions have serious emotional consequences for the people caught up in them. Like Winnie, the elderly heroine of Azzopardi's second novel, the quite as neatly titled *Remember Me*, the junior Gaucis are searching not just for security and peace of mind – all the things that most ordinary people take for granted – but for their own identities, desperately pursuing something that is recognisably their own but more often taking refuge in collective solidarity. The stripped down, collaborative, movie-fuelled slang in which the children converse ('POW Dolores Gauci… Spill the beans'), full of callous public insult and heartfelt private love, is, in its way, a form of protection in which harsh realities are hinted at but rarely openly acknowledged.

In the end the house in Tiger Bay gives up most, if not quite all, of its secrets. We know what happened to Salvatore down at the dockside, and we can follow the movement of the money stolen from his safe. We can explain the provenance of the bank notes under the tea-pot and we can guess something of the way in which Frankie treats his children. The puzzle set for the reader in decoding this tangled web of clues is compounded by the subtlety of the writing style, an outwardly innocuous piling up of very ordinary phrases and descriptions in which unobtrusive special effects lurk far below the surface, like depth charges waiting to go off. The scene in which baby Dolores sits entombed in a room which is about to erupt in flames is a terrific example of Azzopardi's technique – artfully signposted, deviously set up and then adroitly shifting the focus of its horror by concentrating on the world beyond the slammed shut door.

Neatly set out, exactly defined, hard, sharp and visceral, the world of the Gaucis also turns out to be permanently in flux. There are bulldozers out demolishing the slum houses, piles of rubble where shops once stood, and Fran's torching of the local grocers' shop turns out to be a blessing in disguise for its soon to be evicted owners. Many of the characters are eventually revealed to be voyagers in transit, for whom Tiger Bay is simply a stepping stone on some long and unforeseeable journey, far away from Cilla, Dusty or the Searcher's 'Needles and Pins.' Azzopardi can be quietly funny when she wants to – the pre-Frankie Mary, a refugee from bar work in the valleys fetched up in a rather more select establishment, reflects that the exotic selection of drinks on offer wouldn't have done for the patrons of the Penderyn Miners' Welfare, who drank either Mild or Bitter 'depending on how they felt.' But *The Hiding Place*'s predominating tone is wryness, and the rueful banter that covers up its trails is rarely more than camouflage. What really went on hangs slightly out of reach, gathered up in cracks and hideaways, made all the more threatening by the stealthy obliqueness of its glance.

Introduction to Picador Classics edition, 2016

PHILIP CALLOW: ON THE BOHO TRAIL

The Hosanna Man

Back in 1975 the New Fiction Society – a highbrow book club underwritten at calamitous expense by the Arts Council – took out a full-page advertisement in the *Observer* to promote its inaugural list. The ad took the form of a series of portraits, each attached to a starkly interrogative caption. One of these demanded of its subject 'Is this a working-class novelist?' It was a good question, as working-class novelists nearly always turn out to be an unexpectedly heterogeneous bunch, keen to resist the categorisations wished upon them by text books or the smash and grab raids of social historians anxious to fillet their novels for supporting detail.

This differentiation is particularly acute in the decade after the Second World War, a period in which the 'new wave' of working-class literature quickly divides into at least half-a-dozen contending rivulets. There is the anarchic underclass fiction of Alan Sillitoe, Stan Barstow's 'lace-curtain' novels, whose characters tend to be slightly more bourgeois in outlook , John Braine's upwardly mobile materialism (*Room at the Top*, 1957), even a Tyneside branch – see Sid Chaplin's *The Day of the Sardine* – in which adolescent anomie is unravelled against a background of corrupt municipal socialism. And at the very end of the file comes Philip Callow (1924–2007) whose early work, while bearing faint situational resemblances to a book like *Saturday Night and Sunday Morning*, resembles, as Angela Carter once noted, 'nothing but itself.'

Like Sillitoe, Callow's *locus classicus* was the Nottinghamshire East Midlands, but the heroes of his best-known novels –

Common People, say, or the *Another Flesh* trilogy – are usually working-class bohemians, self-educated, naively passionate, less concerned with securing a 'proper' job or a conventional relationship than with living as authentically and intensely as possible. The description of Louis Paul, here in Callow's debut from 1956 – 'I had been wandering about the country for a time, trying to decide what to do with my life, struggling and then drifting with the tide' – could be applied to practically any one of his protagonists, who are defined by their rootlessness and susceptibility to impulse, a perpetual striving rendered all the more poignant by the fact that the thing being striven for hangs eternally out of reach.

The Hosanna Man opens with Louis's arrival in Nottingham, in last-ditch pursuit of a married woman named Stella who has lately put a stop to their relationship and forbidden him to write. And yet in some ways this is a false trail, for Callow's real interest, you deduce, lies not in Louis's tracking down of his former mistress – they meet only once, inconclusively, in the street – but in his efforts to find himself in her absence. These kick into gear when, via a newspaper small ad ('creative, spiritual group looking for financial backing') he gets in with a group of down-at-heel artistic types, to whose charismatic convenor Jack Kelvin, he immediately takes a shine, ('he'll draw people to him because he's alive and kicking.')

Louis's hankering for spiritual renewal, focused on the figure of the wild-eyed backstreet guru, replete with endless talk about the need for new solutions and fresh ways of looking at life, while Tolstoy, Whitman, Nietzsche, Dostoevsky *et al* lurk grimly in the background, soon turns this into a thoroughly representative Fifties artefact. There are, for example, faint points of contact with Angus Wilson's short story 'A Bit off the Map', published a year later, with its mystical genius Huggett (a faithful portrait of Colin Wilson) leader of a group of amateur savants known as 'The Crowd'. The difference between them, though, is one of social level, for Callow's people are not trend-fomenters with one eye on the gossip column of the *Daily Express* but *echt*-bohemians who live in flyblown lodging houses and assemble their daily allowances in half-pence, entirely detached from mainstream existence.

Callow's major influence, inevitably, is D.H. Lawrence, and *The Hosanna Man* fairly bristles with super-charged descriptions of very ordinary things. 'His hair was greased flat on his head, eaten away at the temples like a mouldy fur' Louis notes of an old work colleague. 'The skin of his face was so bloodless it looked evil, startlingly white and somehow soiled and sordid.' His favourite adjective is 'naked.' An electric light, once switched on, strips Louis 'naked where he stands'. Little patches of garden before the terraced houses 'had an almost indecent look to them; they were so naked and exposed.' Meanwhile, our hero's egotism 'ate into me like an acid' and if there is an enemy it can be found in the consumer materialism of radios, cars and vacuum-cleaners that makes Kelvin's *inamorata* Doreen prefer a quiet life with her husband.

If a faint air of portentousness hangs over some of this earnest chatter about art in the bleak East Midlands twilight as the gas meter clicks ominously forward and the walls seem to 'run' with colour, then it is entirely redeemed by Callow's seriousness. He, and his characters, mean what they say, and the living of a meaningful life is far more important to them than such minor considerations as whether or not the floor has a carpet. It is the same with the novel's narrative line, whose 'plot', such as it is, involves little more than Louis sharing a flat with Kelvin, falling in with a friendly bookseller, going to one or two parties and finally meeting a woman with whom he enjoys an again intensely Lawrentian commingling. You don't read Callow to see whether the hero marries the boss's daughter or punches the foreman on the nose; you read him to see what sense, in the end, the he make of his life. The least that can be said in his favour is that while many a Fifties classic now gets filed under 'reportage', *The Hosanna Man* looks like a genuine work of art.

Literary Review, 2014

CHIPS FROM THE NOVELIST'S WORKBENCH

KINGSLEY AMIS – *Complete Stories*

To judge from his published comments, Kingsley Amis had no great opinion of his short stories. The introduction to a collected edition from 1980, which offers some observations on the form, is horribly self-deprecating. The kind of stories he writes, Amis maintains, are 'telescoped novels.' True, there are other kinds ('the impression, the untrimmed slice of life, the landscape without characters' and so on) but these don't appeal. In any case, such items are, we infer, more likely to appear in unread volumes sponsored by the Arts Council. All we are left with, Amis humbly deposes, is a drizzle of 'chips from a novelist's workbench.' By and large critics and biographers have tended to accept this low valuation. Zachary Leader's monumental *The Life of Kingsley Amis* (2006) mentions a bare half-dozen. Richard Bradford's *Lucky Him* (2001) finds space for only four.

All this might seem to discourage a potential anthologist, but *Complete Stories* – two dozen of these chips, written between 1955 and 1993 – is what the Amis-era publishing trade used to call a handsome volume, even if a touch inaccurate in some of its supporting detail. Mysteriously, there is no place for 'Interesting Things', included in *My Enemy's Enemy* (1962). 'Affairs of Death' did not, as the contents page insists, appear in the 1980 volume – it was first published in *Shakespeare Stories* (1982) – and Amis's remarks on the nature of the beast, quoted above, are mis-dated by seven years. What Amis, with his keen eye for editorial laxity, would have made of this can be easily imagined. On the other hand, he would have been reassured by Rachel Cusk's brisk and lapidary introduction ('vigorous observational prose… admirable delicacy… utilitarian beauty') which descries a world made up of 'social frustration, fleshly appetite, critical disquiet and the sometimes painful bridling of personal emotional power.'

This is true, but it is not indefinitely true, and the reader who tackles *Complete Stories* chronologically will notice, among other things, a serious, if incremental, falling off. Not to put too fine a point on it, the early pieces – up until the early 1970s, say – tend to be longer, more 'realistic' and, almost without exception, better written. They are also more rooted in Amis's own experience. 'My Enemy's Enemy' (1955), 'Court of Inquiry' (1956) and 'I Spy Strangers' (1962) cover his war-time adventures in an army Signals unit, plainly derive from 'Who Else is Rank?', the unpublished novel co-written with his fellow-serviceman Frank Coles, and are full of things that actually happened (like Archer in 'Court of Inquiry' Lieutenant Amis managed to lose a charging-engine), real people and private jokes.

'Colonel the Lord Fawcett', who demands a despatch rider for the conveyance of his soiled laundry to Brussels, is transparently based on Colonel the Lord Glenarthur, rated by Amis's *Memoirs* (1991) as 'the biggest shit on the entire staff.' Coles himself is promoted to 'General Coles', commander of the 11/17 Army Corps Group. In much the same way 'Moral Fibre', from 1958, is a souvenir of the Swansea lecturing days, in which Lewis, the hero of *That Uncertain Feeling* (1955), negotiates (as did Amis) some of the problematic ethical territory occupied by a cleaning lady who not only doubles up as a prostitute but offers him an evening's entertainment into the bargain.

All this allows for a variety of theme and treatment. 'My Enemy's Enemy', in which Captain Thurston declines to warn a fellow-officer of a snap inspection, is about moral cowardice. 'I Spy Strangers', set mostly in a soldiers' mock-parliament, whose leftist fervour anticipates the result of the 1945 General Election, is a piece of retrospective teleology, advertising some of the social adjustments of the post-war era ('Something monstrous and indefinable was growing in strength' Major Raleigh decides, 'something hostile to his accent and taste in clothes and modest directorship and ambitions for his sons and redbrick house at Purley with its back-garden tennis-court.') 'Moral Fibre', far more sympathetic to louche, man-eating Betty than her vigilant social worker, is about not being interfered with, a shot across the bows in what was later to become a decades-long engagement with domineering state-ism.

Collectively, though, these early pieces nearly always turn on questions of identity. Their real aim, you suspect, is to establish who, in the last resort, the people wandering about in them really are, and the difficulty of judging or even satisfactorily accounting for their behaviour. Having extricated himself from the Court of Inquiry by throwing himself on the senior officer's mercy ('I'm so sorry to have let you down personally, Major Raleigh. That's what gets me, failing in my duty to you, sir') Archer admits to feigning his distress. Amis's narrator, alternatively, thinks it 'was perhaps questionable whether any amount of ordinary acting talent could have prevented the blushes I had seen.' Who is to know what Archer's true feelings are? Or whether his *confidante* is fit to judge them?

'Moral Fibre', alternatively, moves on from the question of who people really are to wonder about the kind of lives they ought to be leading. No doubt prostitution is a bad thing, Lewis reflects, but Betty seems far happier when recounting her exploits down among the 'business girls' – livelier, sharper, more human even – than when reunited with her stolid Norwegian husband in their run-down flat. It is not that Amis's characters want to avoid moral judgments – nearly all the stories insist on the absolute necessity of moral judgments being made – merely that the materials needed to build up a convincing case for prosecution or defence are always slightly out of reach.

Worse, the situations set in train are often further complicated by subsidiary characters choosing to declare a stance, reveal aspects of themselves or the people around them that either come too late to do any good or have moral implication for those on the receiving end. 'My Enemy's Enemy' skids to a halt with the hitherto unforthcoming Captain Bentham offering Thurston a few home truths about his conduct. 'All the Blood Within Me' (1962) reaches a similarly ambiguous climax when a man attending the funeral of a married woman he has loved for thirty years gets a crisp little lecture from the daughter of the deceased on her failings as a wife and mother.

In nearly every case, lurking in the background is a profound distrust of the institution, even when, as in 'Dear Illusion' (1972), the story of a celebrated poet who repudiates his art, the institution being distrusted is something as vague as 'literature' or 'culture.' The army corrupts, as it subordinates individual intelligence and mutual goodwill to an autocratic norm. The state and its social workers corrupt, as they are more interested in bringing predetermined solutions to human frailties rather than listening to the people experiencing them. As might be expected, the prose style brought to these charge-sheets is one of maximum irony and deflation. Take these two excerpts from 'Court of Inquiry':

> The Mess occupied a Belgian provincial hotel and this was its lounge, a square room lined with burst leather-padded benches. Officers sat on them reading magazines, Only the fact that two or three of them were also drinking stopped the place looking like a barber's waiting room. Outside it was raining a little.
>
> Lunch in the heavily panelled dining room was served by three Belgian waitresses wearing grey dresses and starched aprons. Their ugliness was too extreme to be an effect of chance. Perhaps they had been selected by a burgomagisterial committee as a proof against the most licentious of soldiery. Such efforts would have been wasted. Libido burnt feebly in Raleigh's domain.

The prime influence here is Anthony Powell: not the Powell of

A Dance to the Music of Time (then only in its early stages) but the early novels such as *Venusberg* (1932) and *From a View to a Death* (1933), which Amis recalled having recommended to him by Philip Larkin in wartime Oxford. The Powell connection endured: one of the very last stories, 'Toil and Trouble', has a minor character called Pennistone, presumably in homage to Nick Jenkins' intellectual friend.

Amis seems to have given up on realism, or a carefully stylised approximation of it, sometime in the early 1970s. Thereafter the stories span what Rachel Cusk calls his 'interests and preoccupations. A clump of time-travel vignettes attests to the mid-period fascination with sci-fi. There are Conan Doyle pastiches ('The Darkwater Hall Mystery'), devious literary conceits ('Affairs of Death' finds Macbeth on a visit to the Pope) and an eye-catching exercise in the historical subjunctive, '1941/A', supposedly written by Oxford University's 'Josef Goebbels Professor of History', which describes the successful German-Japanese assault on the United States mainland.

None of them is without interest, or a certain amount of technical pizzazz. On the other hand even Amis die-hards will have trouble with the prose style, which come the late 1980s is in a fairly ramshackle state. 'Toil and Trouble', a credulity-straining affair about the kidnapping of a literary agent, is full of routine phrases and descriptions that don't truly describe: 'well-groomed, well-dressed men of forty' who sit behind large desks writing things; 'unfamiliar, small, clean but barely-furnished' rooms; writers who 'show a relentless determination to stay in touch with the reading public.' It is a continent away from Major Raleigh, who is said to resemble 'more than ever a moustachioed choirboy in battledress.'

There are occasional moments, too, in which Amis looks to be deliberately lessening his range, getting the bull between his sights and then self-consciously settling for an outer. 'Who or What Was It?' (1972) is a bizarre little pendant to *The Green Man* (1969), in which the author and his second wife, Elizabeth Jane

Howard, turn up at a country pub that resembles in certain vital particulars the ghost-ridden establishment of the novel. As Zachary Leader notes in *The Life of Kingsley Amis*, for all its relish of ghost-busting, wish-fulfilment and things that go bump in the night, *The Green Man* is ultimately a realistic account of a man at the end of his tether. Alcoholically at the end of his tether, too, whereas 'Who or What Was It?', which abandons the connection between booze and the paranormal, is much straightforwardly a genre exercise.

No point, of course, in harping on these limitations, as Amis seems to have been perfectly aware of them himself. The Crimea-era radio play 'Captain Nolan's Chance', included here by dint of its appearance in *Mr Barrett's Secret and Other Stories* (1993) is merely the kind of thing that the mature Amis liked to write. Critics and Arts Council subsidy-merchants could go hang. In the end you suspect that the difference between *Complete Stories'* scintillating first 200 pages and the relative mediocrity of what follows is a consequence of the way in which the average literary life gets lived. 'My Enemy's Enemy', 'Moral Fibre' and perhaps another half-a-dozen of the stories assembled here were clearly, as F.R. Leavis might have put it, written out of a pressure of something to be conveyed. The rest offer the not always terribly exciting spectacle of a professional writer getting on with his job.

Times Literary Supplement, 2011

BETWEEN APPOINTMENTS: PIERS PAUL READ

The Misogynist

The most striking thing about Piers Paul Read's early novels was their characters' susceptibility to physical decay. The bloom of youth barely had time to settle before it was over-run by maggots. Thus, coolly appraising his mistress's somewhat faded charms, Hilary Fletcher in *The Upstart* (1973) notes that marriage and children 'had loosened her bones and skin and clouded those once fresh eyes with the film of age.' Harriet, it turns out, is all of 26. Strickland, the barrister hero of *A Married Man* (1979) has an even worse time of it, what with the smell of his wife's wind and 'the liverish early morning odour from her mouth.' Clare, alas, is a long over-the-hill 32.

Read's insistence on the inexorability of human decline was a necessary preamble to his single great theme. This was not simply the vanity of human wishes, but the working out of divine providence. For *The Upstart* and *A Married Man* were Catholic novels, as astringent and remorseless in their way as anything by such previous exponents of the form as Evelyn Waugh and R.H. Benson. The human activity that went on in them, you inferred, had very little significance when set against the much more serious destinies that lurked around the corner. Fletcher, waiting to have tea with his wife and children, while reflecting on his inevitable death, believes that 'between these two appointments there is nothing of importance.'

All this – Fletcher's quietism, the average human existence seen as a kind of tedious sideshow – gestures at the great dilemma of the Catholic novel: a dilemma rendered all the more acute by the fact that most of its practitioners would deny that it even exists.

To Read, the paradox of his work – a scrupulous realism suddenly undercut by irradiations of divine grace – is not a paradox: it is merely evidence of God working his purpose out. *The Upstart*, for example, grinds to a halt when Fletcher, a vengeful vicar's son who has systematically ruined the lives of the aristocratic family in the great house next door – wanders into a prison confessional and repents. No point in the non-believer complaining that the scene is psychologically flawed, that nothing in Fletcher's history gives it plausibility. God works in mysterious ways, you see, and the literary critic can only nod his head.

If *The Misogynist*'s Catholicism takes a certain amount of time to declare itself, then the physical decay is more or less its opening gambit. It could hardly be anything else, as this, broadly speaking, is a novel about late sixty-something *angst*. Jomier, its male lead, is an embittered ex-barrister, whose wife has divorced him for a plutocrat and whose merchant banker son, though dutiful, regards him as a failure. The one bright spot in his life is his daughter Louisa, now married to a wealthy Argentinian and living in distant Buenos Aires. Conscious of his mediocrity, but cannily self-sufficient, Jomier is a great one for spreadsheets, minute financial calculations and (a tribute to his professional beat) argument for argument's sake, and while one sympathises with him in his predicament – growing old in a Hammersmith terrace with the clamour of London resounding in his ears – one sympathises even more with his absconding wife.

Things pick up no end when, as a much valued spare man on the West London dinner circuit – on this evidence slightly superior to an Arctic ice floe in terms of comfort and amenity – Jomier is introduced to (relatively) lissom, yoga-teaching and hard-up Judith. Suppers, highbrow films and earnest conversation soon give way to equally earnest sexagenarian sex, set down with all Read's customary attention to detail ('Her lips are not as plump and cushioning as those of a younger woman; he can feel her teeth beneath her skin' etc) and a Yuletide visit to Venice. Sadly, Judith turns out to be a corking bore on the good brave topics of global warming and meat-eating as well as faintly irked by her paramour's heroic efforts with the expenses ('The provisional figures for the stay at the Hotel Palazzo Solaia now stand at E2,111.59 for Jomier and E1,091.59 for Judith. Working on the premise that Christmas dinner in a good restaurant would have cost E120 a head at the very least, Jomier knocks E300 off the E420, Judith's share of the bundled Christmas dinner, welcome pack etc, but divides the E863.18 for miscellaneous extras by two. This he considers generous…')

Sharply written, mournfully acute on the horrors of twenty-first century London, and unquestionably Read's best novel since *A Season in the West* (1988), *The Misogynist* is also rather an odd book. Part of the oddity lies in Jomier himself, in his innocuousness, his second-rateness, his self-justifying stinginess (see in particular the computation which establishes that Judith is costing him £300 a year in Viagra.) Again, Read would probably deny that this is a drawback. Jomier – peevish, ghost-haunted, selfish – is *l'homme moyen sensuel* personified: who could be more in need of God's grace? Much more of it, though, lies in the novel's eerie resemblance to other exercises in this line by Justin Cartwright. Like Cartwright, Read specialises in present-tense staccato ('Jomier broods. He broods about the present. He broods about the past'), in grand-sounding but debatable statements about human motivation ('Women are all over their husbands and boyfriends until they have had children') in frequent, self-pinioning questions ('Can one be a racist without knowing it, like the carrier of a disease? What is a racist? How is racism to be defined?')

The difference between them is, of course, that spiritual dimension. Throughout Jomier's Viagra-sustained couplings with Judith, the experienced Read-fancier will be waiting for the Catholicism to kick in. By about half-way through the wait becomes unbearable. Will an angel with a flaming sword descend on Jomier's head as he marches gamely to the door of his beloved's Wandsworth semi? Will a modern-day Father D'Arcy drag him into a pew at Farm Street and urge him to recant? In fact, the initial twitch upon the thread comes on the Venice holiday, when, coming out of a midnight mass, Judith clutches his arm and insists that she 'had the feeling the whole thing was genuine.' Then comes a much more serious jolt – the news that kind, God-fearing, Catholic convert Louisa – by far the nicest character in the book – is suffering from a potentially fatal blood disorder. Jomier knows what he has to do: 'He can make deals. If God will save Louisa, he will have his quid pro quo. Jomier will love, believe, repent and forgive.'

God saves Louisa, but he does so, alas, by uncovering yet more deceit and treachery in Jomier's past life. By deflecting this away from the real culprit – his ex-wife – Jomier makes that vital step towards redemption. And this, it seems to me, is the difference between the Mark I Read of *Monk Dawson* (1969) and *The Upstart* and his latest incarnation. Hilary Fletcher walked into a confessional, had his sins expunged and his torment soothed. Jomier has his daughter restored to him at the expense of his pride and, even worse, his paternity. If some of Read's early novels seemed bleak in their conclusions about human frailty, then this is bleaker still. Brooding, candid and unsparing, it is a welcome return to form

The Spectator, 2010

TUGGING FREE FROM THE MOORINGS: PHILIP HENSHER

King of the Badgers

Even for a work that surges unappeasably beyond its 400th page, *King of the Badgers* has a great many individual compartments. There is the abduction of the eight year-old girl that sets the story in motion. There is the North Devon town of Hanmouth, a dozen or so of whose inhabitants are seen cautiously inter-acting beneath the media glare. Then, threatening to swamp the existing plot-lines altogether with the brio of its attack, comes a series of despatches from the modern gay front-line, taking in cheese-vending Sam and his lordly boyfriend Harry, David, the fat, unhappy son of one of Hanmouth's modestly retired couples, and an entire gang of rorting south-western party-planners known as The Bears.

And finally, looming above the proceedings like a triumphal arch, there is the conversation. Like Angus Wilson, a possible influence on these scenes from provincial life, Hensher's forte is the social round: the party; the conversation in the grocer's shop; the fragments of repartee borne back on the high street breeze. One of the best chapters switches from a housewarming bash at the home of David's parents, colonised and then forsaken by various of the Bears prior to their own private orgy. The Hanmouth habitués prattle on endlessly, and, as with the cast of Hensher's previous novel, the Booker-shortlisted *The Northern Clemency*, not everything they say is strictly to the point. Along with the fragments of repartee borne back on the high street breeze lurks the faint scent of desultoriness.

The occasional hint of an endeavour that has begun to tug free from its original moorings extends to the story-line. It begins with the vanished girl and a scenario of collusion and familial fracture borrowed from the Shannon Matthews case. All this – the press photographers paddled across the estuary, the conniving mother, the paranoid public meetings – is brilliantly done, and yet there is a way in which Hensher seems to lose interest in it, veering off about half-way through into a rapt conspectus of brigadiers and their wives, seconded Treasury officials and their secrets and West Country rough trade that leaves poor, defiled China someway behind.

In procedural terms, you can see Hensher's point. China, together with her flint-eyed mum and idiot step-dad are there to represent something – a social tendency or a media fixation. His quirkier characters, on the other hand, are allowed space to luxuriate. Again, like its predecessor, *The King of Badgers* runs to half-a-dozen memorable scene-swellers: teenaged Hettie, with her passionate friendships and her collection of dolls (these have names like 'Shitface' and 'Child Pornography'); the sinister and ventriloquial Mr Calvin; David's Italian chum Mauro and his light-fingered way with the household ornaments. The funny-horrible – see Angus Wilson, once again – is much in evidence, notably in a scene in which David, returning to London in high dudgeon, leaves Mauro in the car while he repairs to a motorway diner for a burger jamboree, only to meet his end over a line of coke in the gents.

As ever one is struck, and seduced, by a coruscating intelligence that manifests itself in dozens of literary allusions waiting to be uncombed (the character who, when shamed 'that the town in which she had made her home had not, it seemed, wanted a butcher,' gestures at the last line of Penelope Fitzgerald's *The Bookshop*), and hundreds of individual sentences burnished up to the max. 'On the quay a senior policeman stood' Hensher writes at one point: nine out of ten novelists would have written 'stood a senior policeman' and lost the rhythm. To be sure, some of the intelligence is a matter of Hensher asserting his own personality – telling us, for example, what he thinks about mobile-users on trains or the teaching of creative writing in provincial universities. It has to be said, too, that certain of the characters have a tendency to wilt beneath his penetrating eye: the compassion goes only so far.

As to what *King of the Badgers* is 'about', its real theme is neither child abduction, provincial life or even the south-west England gay leisure experience, but the loss of individual and collective freedoms. Mr Calvin, whose neighbourhood watch committee is shown to consist entirely of himself, is rather too obviously named. There is far too much sheer detail in it – too many descriptions of the bijou artefacts on display in gay drawing-rooms, and too many sedulous dinner menus ('an elegantly refined imitation of a shepherd's pie with Italian *ragu* and celeriac in the mash' etc). In mitigation, Hensher is one of the few English novelists at work who is a) seriously interested in the varieties of modern Englishness, and b) has the intellectual resources to address them. All this makes the occasional near-Olympian fussiness of his technique very easy to forgive.

Independent, 2011

JULIAN BARNES'S STUFF

Pulse

Some years ago at the King's Lynn Fiction Festival I watched Julian Barnes being interviewed by the late Beryl Bainbridge. It was an instructive sight. 'The thing about your books, Julian' pronounced Dame Beryl, who had perhaps taken a glass of wine, 'is that they're all about *death*.' This is true, of course, but Barnes's work has a second fixation. This is its line on *stuff*. If anything gives the 14 stories in this patchy new collection a unifying link, it is their fascination with what might be called the humdrum materials of existence: the everyday routines and preoccupations which tether his characters to their lives, and can sometimes – 'stuff' being as uncontrollable as knotgrass on a lawn – severely limit their room for manoeuvre.

A sentence in 'Gardeners' World' gestures at the way in which the Barnes short story works. Ken, its eight-years-married co-star, has been given a soil-testing kit by his wife. 'pH, he learnt, was a number used to express degrees of acidity or alkilinity in solutions, formerly the logarithm to base 10 of the reciprocal of the concentration of hydrogen ions, but now related by formula to a standard solution of potassium hydrogen phthalate, which has value 4 at 15 degrees centigrade.' The reader already knows that all this – the dibbers, the wodgers, the Ursula Buchan primers – is bearing a huge metaphorical weight on its shoulders, but he will also suspect that Barnes, being a stuff merchant, can't resist all that enticing detail about leafcurl and black spot, while noting that, stuck in this figurative jungle, Ken and his wife are going to have to struggle to achieve any kind of life of their own.

It is the same with 'Trespass', which is about rambling in the countryside, and 'East Wind' (estate agent hero) which only just escapes the longing embrace of its property gazetteer ad-ons ('1930s semi, pebbledash, multi-occupation, metal windowframes rusting up badly' Vernon notes of his beloved's bedsit.) These are tight, rueful and almost desperately ironic stories whose characters are in permanent danger of being engulfed by the things they do. So Geoff in 'Trespass', taking his ladyfriend out on exacting route-marches, seems a much less solid proposition than the 'Bowden Bridge car park, the reservoir, pick up the Pennine Way to the Downfall, right at Red Brook' itinerary that Barnes has duly filched from the OS map. The scenery is somehow more arresting than the man marching laboriously through it.

Or perhaps, in a way, this is Barnes's point, and the thraldom in which his characters are held by their environment is quite deliberate. The people in *Pulse* are a ground-down lot: resigned divorcees (the phrase 'he didn't mind one way or the other' recurs); the world-weary middle-aged, lately arrived at the peak of life's parabola and now careening down the other side. Life, thinks Alice, the ageing writer in 'Sleeping with John Updike', is 'the gradual loss of pleasure.' Self-destructive tendencies abound, and can rarely be kept in check. 'Was it that, deep down, he had an urge to fuck everything up?' broods Vernon in 'East Wind', as he legs off in pursuit of the stolid East European café waitress. Ultimately Vernon goes too far, discovers the secret of his girlfriend's buried life and is summarily abandoned.

Short stories nearly always suffer from being assembled in volume form. The reader starts to see the joins, work out how the tricks are played, look on knowingly as the next artful metaphor begins to uncoil, and in this particular case to wonder whether the Trades Descriptions Act couldn't usefully be invoked. The four 'At Phil and Joanna's' pieces are simply exercises in the higher banter, smart-alecky conversations of the kind that presumably illumine North London dining-rooms after the children have gone to bed. By the more exacting definitions, 'Complicity' and

'Carcassonne' hardly count as short stories – just Barnes delightedly retailing interesting facts he has picked up and joining one or two of life's vagrant dots slyly together.

When the absorption in subject matter can be overcome, on the other hand, things really starts to shift. 'East Wind' gathers its figurative threads up into a single, spectacular knot with Vernon, staring once more out of the café window and finding the view the same 'except that there used to be a row of beach huts… Then someone had burnt them down.' 'Marriage lines' is a haunting sketch of a newly-widowed man returning to the Scottish island where he and his wife went annually on holiday. In 'The Limner' Barnes turns in an atmospheric historical piece about a deaf-mute Yankee portrait-painter, while in the title story he subdues an understandable temptation to luxuriate in the detail of his hero's evenings at the running club to offer a nicely observed account of a young man's marriage failing against the backdrop of his parents' declining health. The jury is still out on that eternal debate about Barnes the essayist *manqué*, but it is a fact that what weakens the less successful stories in *Pulse* is their surfeit of information.

Financial Times, 2010

III. PORTRAITS

DOWN AMONG THE HERBIVORES: ALAN BENNETT

Keeping On Keeping On

It's a mark of Alan Bennett's centrality to the modern literary scene that he manages to turn up in the consciousness of the averagely bookish person at the rate of two or three times a week. And so, in the five days it took me to read this lavish miscellany I found myself inundated, surrounded and in the end positively menaced by references to him in other books and art-forms. There he was in a battered anthology from the early days of the *London Review of Books* appraising a volume of reminiscences by his old hero (and star of his first big dramatic hit, *Forty Years On*) Sir John Gielgud. There he was again in the paperback of the second tranche of Charles Moore's biography of Mrs Thatcher swelling the throng of her very substantial band of book-world detractors. And there he was for a third time in the DVD of Channel Four's late '90s attempt on Anthony Powell's *A Dance to the Music of Time*, playing the part of Sillery, the conniving Oxford don.

Each of these fleeting appearances turned out to be characteristic of a personality that *Keeping on Keeping On* sets in sometimes uncomfortably sharp relief. The Gielgud review finds him appreciative, nostalgic and also hugely funny (of the censoriousness of the bygone Brighton theatre goers, he notes that 'The sleek Sussex matrons sit poised in the stalls like greyhounds in the slips. The first 'fuck' and they're a mile down the sea front, streaking for Hove.') *Mrs Thatcher: The Authorised Biography*, on the other hand, showcases a seriously affronted Bennett, loudly disparaging his *bete noire*'s reading of a Larkin poem and, as Charles Moore discreetly observes, filing his own misinterpretation of the piece's import. The Sillery portrait is the most beguiling of all: fussy, mild-mannered, but altogether failing to disguise deep reservoirs of Powellian tenacity and will-power – qualities that might easily be attributed to Bennett himself.

The least that can be said of *Keeping On Keeping On* is that it is an extraordinarily long book: over 700 pages of play scripts (*Denmark Hill, The Hand of God*), introductions thereunto, *eloges* delivered at funerals, quite half of whose outsize length is given over to a decade's worth (2005–2015) of diaries. The Bennett who emerges from these prodigal jottings, annually extracted by the *LRB*, is a number of things – a loyal friend, a good liberal, a practised sceptic, the proud supporter of many a good brave cause, a brisk observer of the teeming world beyond the Primrose Hill window – but he is above all a complainer, an ingrate of such indefatigable persistence as to straightaway claim a place at a table otherwise reserved for such masters of the art as Larkin, Kingsley Amis and possibly James Lees-Milne.

No doubt about it, the life of a distinguished elderly playwright (Bennett is nearing 71 when the diaries begin), doing the rounds of the rehearsal studios both here and abroad, inspecting country houses in the company of his long-term partner Rupert or simply pottering around the bourgeois end of Camden, is plainly the purest hell. There is the prospect of the Olympic Games ('…I have yet to speak to one person who enthused about the Olympics. If the scenes of ritual rejoicing ('Yes!') were not enough to put one off there is the prospect of seven years of disruption, procrastination, excuses and inconvenience…') There is the fan-mail (like 'being pelted with small stones' apparently) and there is the smugness of the local middle-classes who go around 'hugging themselves in self-congratulation at the perfection of their lives.'

Gradually, as year succeeds year, this net of objurgation extends to take in what celebrity can do for you and what it can't do for you and the cake that can be had and eaten in transit too (sometimes, as when people are being helpful at airports, literally in transit.) Understandably, it hovers over slights – real or imagined – to one's reputation (there is a rueful little entry from 2 September 2006 when someone on *Saturday Review* charges the novelist Mark Haddon with an 'Alan Bennett-ish tweeness' and another one on 7 July 2007 after Terry Eagleton writes a piece in the *Guardian* alleging that 'of all the eminent writers and playwrights only Pinter continues radical and untainted by the Establishment') and is regularly sent forth to pinion mistakes made by journalists over which member of the Cambridge Footlights said what to whom back in, as it may have been, 1959.

Best of all are one or two circular flights of truculence – or perhaps that isn't quite the right phrase for a process in which Bennett seems almost to be policing himself from one sentence to the next, reigning in his outward satisfaction with a whinge and then glossing the whinge in a way that undermines the whole basis of the exercise. There is a wonderful, and wonderfully comic, moment in summer 2013 when Bennett commends the spectacle of streets cleared of traffic by Andy Murray's appearance in the Wimbledon men's single's final. Not, he hastens to assure us, that he is a fan of Murray ('…it's depressing to find his grim grimacing determination has paid off, a triumph of grit over grace.') Then comes a lightning switch from particular to general ('not that anyone in tennis has much grace these days') followed by a brisk cancelling out of the author's qualifications for making his judgments in the first place ('as if I knew [or cared]')

Check. Counter-check. Counter-counter-check. With Larkin, or Amis, or a good many other diarists and letter-writers who give ballast to a life by listing its irritations, this would be simple peevishness. Here the effect is heightened, or occasionally mitigated, by the reader's suspicion that Bennett is rather too aware of the effect that today's disquiet will be causing to tomorrow's reader, and that rather more is going on here than initially meets the eye – another connection, perhaps, between Bennett the dramatist and Bennett the journal keeper and intermittent man-of-letters. This, though, is comic. Much less larky in their collective impact are the howitzer volleys of *J'accuses* aimed at prime ministers, governments, bureaucrats, media tycoons, environmental despoilers and practically anyone opposed to 'that blend of backward-looking radicalism and conservative socialism which does duty for my political views.'

This may be a statement of ideological intent, but it also hints, however indirectly, at a kind of socio-cultural positioning. In strict category terms Bennett is what used to be known as a 'herbivore', a bright child of the 1930s sent out into the world in the early post-war era and, by extension, the beneficiary of such lasting social and intellectual influences as grammar schools, Oxbridge, National Service, the Third Programme and the Penguin Specials – in Bennett's case given a decisive twist by his resolute northerness (if Mrs Thatcher was the grocer's daughter from Grantham, then this is the butcher's son from Leeds) and his homosexuality. The diary carries several references to Richard Hoggart's *The Uses of Literacy*, a classic herbivore text, of which Bennett (born 1934) makes the astute point that for a book published in 1957 and purporting to reflect the realities of its day, it belongs more to the world of his parents than his own upbringing in wartime Armley.

Another light on the kind of post-war animal that Bennett imagined himself to be can be found in the tribute (again, first published in the *LRB*) to his old Oxford tutor, the medievalist K.B. McFarlane. If Bennett, who spent several years researching and lecturing at Oxford before the satire boom of the early '60s offered a more enticing upward path, and at one point even unsuccessfully sat the All Souls exams, clearly found McFarlane hard going at times, then there is a pointed comparison with the other Magdalen history dons, A.J.P. Taylor and Harry Wheldon. Both of these gentlemen, Bennett recalled, envisaged history as 'a skating rink on which they could show off their techniques, turn their paradoxes...' The note recurs when he sits down to reflect on the TV version of *Wolf Hall*. 'Hilary Mantel, Niall Ferguson, Alan Taylor: History is a playground. The facts are Lego. Make of them what you will.'

Naturally, Bennett is fond of tumbling the Lego around himself: what dramatist isn't? Meanwhile the backward-looking radicalism strays into several areas which other backward-looking radicals might want to contest. It is perfectly possible, for example, to assume – as Bennett frequently does – that the rot set into British public life around about 1980, without also assuming – as Bennett occasionally seems to imply that not everyone who voted for Mrs T was simply greedy or opportunistic. And then there is the case of the actor Chris Langham, imprisoned for downloading child pornography onto his computer, of whom Bennett notes that it worries him when people are prosecuted merely for looking at things – an exemplary liberal sentiment which ignores the fact that a great many children end up being abused because online voyeurs are prepared to pay money to see it done.

One notes this inconsistency not only for the wider moral point, but for the narrower reason that Bennett himself is generally such a well-informed tour-guide to the state of childhood. The young man who appears in the introduction to *Cocktail Sticks*, which again looks back to '40s-era Armley, is in his way another version of a 'type' that exists at the heart of *The Uses of Literacy* – the humbly-born scholarship boy who inhabits a kind of pontoon bridge between the world that forged him and the sleeker landscapes beyond and ends up giving offence to both. Re-reading his letters home from Oxford, and later New York, written in a 'self-consciously homely tone which revived the extremes of dialect and 'Leeds talk' long after my parents had begun to discard them themselves', Bennett admits to being 'ashamed' of his condescension.

And so, like a long, panoramic film, this update on life *Au côte de chez Bennett* winds on, through enough book-signings and jolly suppers with 'Debo D.' to convict our man of a very faint interest in the *beau monde*, through neighbourly chats with Jonathan Miller, chance encounters with everyone from Morrissey to Denis Healey and the visits of the Jehovah's Witnesses, at whose arrival beyond the unopened door Bennett simply lies flat on the carpet until they move on. It is an axiom that the older writers become the more the more they write like themselves, but *Keeping On Keeping On* is so full of sentences that only Bennett could have written that after a bit I started writing them down:

- I never thought buying a tarpaulin, which I did today, could be such a pleasure.
- Roy Keane has the face of a mercenary. Meet him before the walls of fifteenth-century Florence and one's heart would sink.
- 'It's good to talk' is the most specious and misleading injunction since 'All you need is love.'

Absolute highlight here, though, is a passage from the diaries dated 25 January 2007 which begins 'I've taken to eating the occasional date, though it's not a fruit I wholly like.' There follows a reminiscence of 'Mam' buying them when the diarist was young, 'in small compressed bricks', an added attraction being that they went unrationed. Now, who does this sound like? Curiously enough, it sounds remarkably like the aged W.E. Gladstone who, when once offered a bowl of nuts for dessert, observed in an ecstasy of self-absorption that 'It is many years since I ate a Brazil Nut, or indeed any kind of nut.' I'm not sure that Bennett realises quite how funny this is, in the way he seems to appreciate that his niggling over Andy Murray might be. Elsewhere he accuses himself of 'banging on' rather a lot during the year lately concluded, but then this, necessarily, is what diarists do and one might as well tax Anthony Powell (another of Bennett's heroes) with too great an interest in the Old Etonian register. On the other hand, every so often there comes a paragraph about Richard Hoggart or the McFarlane memorial and you forgive him everything. Or nearly everything.

Prospect, 2016

SYBILLE BEDFORD AT THE FEAST

SELINA HASTINGS – *Sybille Bedford: An Appetite for Life*

Thirty years ago, waiting to take my seat at a dinner at the PEN Club in Chelsea, London, I caught sight of an elderly woman quietly installing herself a place or two down on the other side of the long oak table. Though frail and diminutive, there was something rather formidable about this apparition, something steely and self-possessed, and the sense of inner fires, steeply banked increased when she reached into her leather satchel, brought out a bottle of wine, decanted some of it expertly into a glass and began lapping it up like a cat let loose on a saucer of milk. 'That' the person standing next to me murmured, in the manner of one who draws attention to some rare antique run to earth amongst a shelf-full of low-budget curios, 'is Sybille Bedford.'

At this stage in her long and eventful life, Bedford (1911–2006) was luxuriating in the success of *Jigsaw* (1989) which, somewhat implausibly, had been shortlisted for the previous year's Booker Prize for fiction. The implausibility lay in the book's autobiographical tendencies – a tethering in the circumstances of the author's rackety early life in Continental Europe so pronounced that it seemed odd that no judge had wondered whether calling it a novel was an offence against the Trade Descriptions Act for a work whose every other character has an alter-ego purposefully at large on the wrong end of the pre-war French Riviera. 'I thought, you know, that novelists were supposed to make things up' Kingsley Amis once complained, when the full extent of his friend Anthony Powell's failings in this line were revealed to him, and the same charge could be levelled at the little old lady of the PEN Club.

When it came to cannibalising her own life for the purposes of fiction, Bedford, like Powell, was a serial offender, a kind of literary anthrophage forever feasting on her own lightly grilled bones. In this comprehensive and admiring biography, Selina Hastings notes that in *Jigsaw*, subtitled *An Unsentimental Education*, her subject's fourth novel, 'the difference between reality and imagination is almost impossible to discern.' But the same critique can be made of her second, *A Favourite of the Gods* (1963) – 'a mirror image of Sybille's adolescence' according to Hastings. It hangs ominously over her third, *A Compass Error* (1968), large parts of which simply recapitulate material from the previous volume, and it doubtless explains the distressing family sit-down of 1956 when after publication of her debut, *A Legacy*, a posse of Sybille's German relatives turned up in London to protest at the pain that this 'ghastly book' had caused them.

Sybille, in short, was not only an autobiographer *manqué*, but a recycler and a re-animator, to the point where her work, seen in the round, sometimes looks like a gigantic palimpsest, a constantly re-stitched piece of embroidery, a single idea endlessly refashioned and refurbished, the same remorseless tocsin clanging away above her readers' heads. All this suggests that the experience on which her books were based is of a highly unusual, or highly stylised, kind, and that the living of it at once defined her as a creative artist and yet channelled that creativity into a groove that she could not have escaped even had she wanted to. There were to be no flights of fancy, capricious experiments, or attempts to break new ground – all the random ballast by which the average literary life is sustained – for the ground already broken was quite fanciful enough to begin with.

So what is *Sybille Bedford: An Appetite for Life* actually about? As well as covering the ups and downs of a high-end, twentieth-century literary career, it is, necessarily, about locales, and journeys and sensations – driving across the Italian border to Alba, let us say, for the truffle season, taking 'a nice walk into

86

empty Belgrave Square', looking for 'a quiet refuge where one can work undisturbed through the summer.' Given the subject's enthusiastic lesbianism, practised without cease over a period of nearly 70 years, it is, naturally, about women – Allanah and Eda and Esther, Betsy and Lesley and Anne – about being taken up, taken out and intermittently taken in. It is about food and drink – white wines with a good smoked salmon mousse and hot toast, *entrecôte grillé, pommes frites* and Fleurie served *frais*, goose *foie gras* – and frequently about judgment ('Life is so much less joyful when you are not there'), even if the most rigorous eye of all sometimes seems to be trained on the *table d'hôte*. Happily the *foie gras* mentioned above turns out to be 'almost unbearably good... It was like a pain to eat the last of it.'

But Hastings' account of this extravagant journey through a succession of gentlewomanly bedrooms and enticing trattoria is something more than a Sapphic carousel with Michelin stars attached. It is also a study of Bohemianism, and what happens to Bohemianism when it grows old. Even more important, perhaps, it is a book about two, or possibly even three demographics that no longer exist. Simultaneously, it offers a series of glimpses into an Old Europe so recondite that to examine it in detail is the social equivalent of inspecting the collection of objects laid out on the raree-showman's table at a Victorian gypsy fair. If Bedford is invariably herself – sharp (at any rate in her later days), self-willed and self-preserving – then she is always, in her highly individual way, a representative of several older worlds that every so often loom into view like slides dragged under a microscope. Like a foregrounded figure in a medieval frieze, her existence is undetachable from the backdrops she seems to dominate.

One of these backdrops is the landscape of her upbringing as the daughter of what Hastings calls 'an eccentric Bavarian baron' on an estate south of Munich. The patronym was 'von Schoenbeck', but there was Jewish blood, acquired through her mother, Lisa, and a fair amount of paternal eccentricity. Keen on *objets d'art*, but notoriously hard-up, the baron seems to have survived on hand-outs from the wealthy parents of his dead first wife. Certainly, Hastings' accounts of life at the schloss at Feldkirch in the aftermath of the Great War sound as if they were robbed wholesale from a novel by Joseph Roth. The von Schoenbecks did not get on and divorced in 1922. Raised mostly by her father, and transferred to her mother's care after his death, Sybille found herself confronted with both a new parent and a new lifestyle. Having spent the first stretch of her teens in the sequestration of a South German village, she spent the second half as a sort of cosmopolitan vagrant, either following Lisa around various European watering holes or being farmed out as a paying guest on people she barely knew.

Eventually mother and daughter fetched up at Sanary-sur-Mer on the French Mediterranean, not far from St Tropez but less fashionable and cheap. And here a second lost landscape looms into view – the world of the inter-war artists' colony, populated by continental drifters drawn south by sunshine, a favourable exchange-rate and a place to work, or to pretend to do so; the kind of place where the car pulled up outside the bistro is pretty sure to contain Aldous Huxley and his wife Maria, and Cyril Connolly is rumoured to be staying in the next village. It takes the description of Sanary, and all the other places in which Sybille spent her peripatetic adolescence, to establish just how odd this early life was, how random, how infinitely detached from 1930s convention. Large parts of it were spent on her own, the solitary girl hunkered down over a book (or the wine-list) in the corner of a out-of-season hotel while Lisa mooned after Nori, the man who became her second husband, or in London bedsitters under the notional eye of English friends. If Sybille relished her independence, then she was also aware of some of its problems. *Jigsaw*, in particular, is weighed down with stealthy intimations of disquiet, sometimes amounting to menace. Here are some specimen sentences:

France became the nearest thing I'd ever known to a home.

I accepted what I found.

Circumstances allowed me to make a choice when I was still incapable of weighing what the choice involved.

That was the beginning of a time of confusion, sudden journeys, new places – waiting – where did we go, and in what order? And who went and who came?

She stayed away for what seemed a long time.

'She', predictably, is Lisa. In each case, you sense that Sybille is pulling her punches, twisting inference around a formal statement of the facts, letting the reader burrow down to the emotional disturbance that lies beneath. If some of the friend she made in the Sanary wine-bars were high-calibre arts world movers and shakers (the Huxleys, Klaus Mann), then others were scene-swelling scamps such as Brian Howard, the part model for Anthony Blanche in Evelyn Waugh's *Brideshead Revisited* (1945). After one particularly raucous evening had ended in a brawl, Howard sent Sybille and her current paramour a verse apology that began: 'With humble gratitude and lowered eyes/Aware of folly, swearing to be wise/No longer tipsy, ribald or inept/The beastliest men in England, we accept.' Meanwhile, one or two of the implications of Sybille's status, or rather her non-status, were becoming uncomfortably clear. As a Jew, her German citizenship was revoked by the Nazis in 1935. Walter Bedford, whom she married in London in 1935, sight unseen, was employed at a gentleman's club in St James's. His later activities are unrecorded. The marriage, contrived by well-placed friends as a way of furnishing her with a British passport, was very nearly forestalled by the Home Office. There were other anxious moments five years later when she and her lover Allanah Harper found themselves stranded on the Riviera as the German tanks sped south. Weighed down by a baggage train that included Allanah's 19 suitcases and the latter's pet poodle, they managed to escape into Italy and board the last passenger ship leaving Genoa for the

United States. Also stowed in the *SS Exeter*'s hold alongside Allanah's compendious reticule was half the Italian gold reserves.

* * * * * * * * * *

It is not the fault of Selina Hastings, always a resourceful and diligent sleuth, that the second half of this 400 page biography is a bit less interesting than the first and its subject not quite so alluring a figure. Perhaps it is just that the gaining of experience nearly always has the edge on its conjuring into print. Back in Europe, not without procedural difficulty (three Dexedrine a day at one point) or emotional distraction ('falling rather madly in love'), she began her literary career with a Mexican travelogue (*The Sudden View*, 1952). Celebrity fans of *A Legacy*, four years later, included Nancy Mitford and Waugh, who wondered, teasingly, who this 'Mrs Bedford' could be ('A cosmopolitan military man, plainly, with a knowledge of parliamentary government and popular journalism, a dislike of Prussians, a liking for Jews, a belief that everyone speaks French in the home.') There was a new lover, Eda, a successor to Evelyn, who had showered Sybille with excruciating twee love letters, in which the pair masqueraded as tortoises, hares and other masculine fauna ('...and all time thinking lovingly of his dearest creature... his GREAT BEAST. SO kind...') and a lucrative side-line reporting such high-profile court cases as the trials of the alleged serial killer Dr Bodkin Adams, the Profumo affair's Stephen Ward, Lee Harvey Oswald's killer Jack Ruby and the gaolers of Auschwitz.

Did success spoil her? Allanah certainly thought so, and Hastings quotes a pained letter from the early 1970s in which she complains that 'You were much nicer and funnier years ago Sibbie, before all the *femme de lettres* stuff.' On the other hand, it may be that this glacial, disdainful side, which other friends also came to bemoan, was a product of Alannah's own sage counsel. Having introduced her to one or two notabilities in Rome in the '50s, Alannah protested that she could not 'understand why you behave like a maid being interviewed when you first meet people... Behaving with ease and a certain boldness on meeting new people, whoever they are... [is] a class thing, and for a person of your breeding and obvious upper-class and even aristocratic family... [your manner] is impossible. It gives people the wrong impression about you.'

Clearly lessons were learned as the grand manner which Sybille seems to adopted by her middle years brought impressive results. Publishers, for example, were consistently cowed by her refusal to be edited, work to deadlines, listen to polite suggestions or submit to all the other minor inconveniences of this exacting trade. Commissioned by *Life* to cover the Auschwitz trial in 1965, she lamented that 'there is this new thing of interfering with writers which is taking on truly frightening dimensions. Have we forgotten that it is writers, original writers not hirelings, who change and make and breathe life into language, not the editors with their levelling tools who limp behind?' Robert Gottlieb, the American publisher who commissioned her life of Huxley (two volumes, 1973–4), was bombarded with snooty letters demanding an advance commensurate with 'my standing as a writer' and a veto on any editorial intervention whatever ('No nagging... no showing of sample chapters... no hurrying.') As a final insult Sybille called in a literary agent halfway through the writing and instructed him to renegotiate the contract.

Another of Sybille's sticking points was having to pay for the expenses racked up while writing 'the biography of one of the world's most distinguished men of letters.' Once the book was out she turned suddenly world-weary and indifferent ('This whole business of publication... is more shocking than I expected. One feels exposed.') *Life* backed down, agreed that Sybille could write at the length she chose and even upped the fee from $3,500 to $5,000. But not everyone was prepared to act as the *en bas* to Sybille's *de haut*, and Hastings offers a choice account of an evening spent with the artist David Hockney in 1978 at the close of which, after being commanded to ferry her home and being further instructed that the corner of Old Church Street wouldn't do ('You will drive me to my door') he returned to ask his host 'Who the fuck is that old bitch?' Meanwhile, the life, now being lived in London, went on as it always had done. There were more girls – Jenny and Annie and Carla and countless others, as undifferentiated, for all Hastings' best efforts, as the faces in a chorus line – and even excursions to a low-rent lesbian club where the talent made itself available by the hour. Asking one of the girls what she did, Sybille was told that she worked 'on the forecourt.' Was this something to do with the Inns of Court, her patron enquired. No, the girl replied, it was a gas station.

There was also a lot more food. Plates of it, banquettes of it, buffets of it, a kind of eternal restaurant groaning with *bouillabaisse*, racks of lamb, cunningly finessed artichokes, roulettes of fillets of sole and sea urchins in aspic. You can forgive Sybille her relish of the high style of these latter days (much of it financed by wealthy friends) as it contrasts so painfully with the insecurity of what had gone before. There is, frankly, something inevitable in a trajectory that finds the one-time bohemian expatriate rooting for Mrs Thatcher, the friend of all those mid-century modernists disliking their post-modern successors (see some wounding remarks about the 'pedestrian and resentful Indian writer' Salman Rushdie) and the émigré from Nazi Germany deciding that 'some races are superior or inferior to others in terms of human development.' It is all of a piece with the Coutts and Co. bank account, the Companionship of the Royal Society of Literature and the *daube a la provencale* with pasta *maconarade*.

If the white wine is nearly always passable, the *entrecôte grillé* impeccable and the partridges perfectly roasted, then with Bedford herself a final judgment hangs slightly out of reach. No point in assailing her hankering for the high life, for sybaritism of this kind has to be worked at, and *la dolce vita* never came easy. Her writing is full of odd, subdued half-lights, the meaning somehow fugitive and ulterior, little hints of bygone unhappiness and life not taking the shape that imagination has wished on it. *Jigsaw* is crammed with these moments – 'Billi' (Sybille) on the beach with her mother at Naples, as the pair of them wonder if 'Alessandro' (Nori) will ever come back. For the first time, the narrator decides, she 'felt the sting of compassion. I never forgot that afternoon by a grey Mediterranean.' As for *An Appetite for Life*, with its stupendous cuisine, its tortoises, hares and great beasts, its disdain for sample chapters and its certain boldness, if not perhaps setting out with this aim in view, Selina Hastings has written a comic masterpiece.

The New Criterion, 2021

ANGELA'S ASHES

ANNE HALL – *Angela Thirkell: A Writer's Life*

De mortuis nil nisi bonum never seemed to apply to Angela Thirkell. The appearance of a full-length biography – Margot Strickland's *Portrait of a Lady Novelist* – 16 years after her death in 1961 triggered a kind of orgy of execration among British reviewers in which a single epithet recurred. To Hilary Spurling in the *Observer*, Thirkell was 'a monstrous egotist, snobbish, reactionary, irredeemably callous in private, mistress in public of the sour aside and the spiteful dig.' The *Listener*'s Patricia Beer, praised a related book, the autobiography of Thirkell's son Graham, for providing 'such a brilliant portrait of a monster in a landscape.' 'A monster, I decided' *The Spectator*'s Francis King recalled of his first meeting with the author of *Cheerfulness Breaks In* (1940) – part of an *oeuvre* no fewer than three-dozen strong, a quick headcount reveals – 'and no subsequent meeting caused me to modify this initial view of her.' To Claire Tomalin in the *Sunday Times*, she was 'unblessed by either gentleness or charity.'

As serial disparagements go, this is quite a catalogue. To it might be appended the headline that introduced Arthur Marshall's *Sunday Telegraph* notice – 'Beast in Tweeds.' Clearly, racking up this level of posthumous scorn requires genius of a sort, not to mention staying-power, and one of the many revelations of Anne Hall's new study of Thirkell is quite how early the rebarbativeness set in. Was there ever a more precocious child sent wandering through the drawing-rooms of late-Victorian England to baffle those present with her smart remarks? Hall quotes a particularly eye-catching exchange between the four-and-a-half year-old Angela and her mother, Margaret McKail's, which must have taken place shortly before Queen Victoria's Diamond Jubilee:

> ANGELA: Bapapa [her grandfather] is your father – your father and your true-hearted love.

> MARGARET: He is.

> ANGELA: But I wonder whom he loves best: me perhaps because I have imp ways and you haven't.

Mrs McKail's reaction to this infant snub is not recorded. Neither is her own mother's response to being told by her three year-old grand-daughter, to whom it had been politely suggested that 'Enough is as good as a feast', that 'Enough wants more.' 'Bapapa' was the distinguished artist Sir Edward Burne-Jones, and it may be that the novelist in waiting was simply enflamed by the grandeur of her associations. She grew up in a pre-Raphaelite oasis in South Kensington, haunted by the ghosts of Watts and Millais, with the future Prime Minister Stanley Baldwin a cousin and Rudyard Kipling a family connection. Sargent drew her portrait – winsome, wistful and oddly inward-looking – J.M. Barrie was her godfather, and the list of her mother's aristocratic friends would fill several pages of *Debrett*.

The early chapters of Anne Hall's concise yet lavishly illustrated biography return us once again to that queer, early twentieth-century West London painters' world, introverted, sequestrated, greenery-yallowy, yet connected to half-a-dozen other landscapes of wealth, prestige and entitlement, where countesses lurk on the stairs, bohemia is acknowledged but not indulged and art rarely has any trouble in paying the rent. The reviewers of *Portrait of a Lady Novelist* were irked, above all, by Angela's treatment of her children – was it not tactless and cruel for her to have insisted that her second husband should beat his two stepsons really hard? – but as *Angela Thirkell: A Writer's Life* makes clear in spades most of the relationships in which she was involved are characterised by an odd chilliness, an inability to make the right judgments, to separate out what seemed suitable and appropriate from what was actually wanted or needed. Her first marriage to a professional singer named John McInnes – bisexual and alcoholic – foundered sometime during the Great War ('*WIFE'S LIFE OF HORROR: Husband's Boasts of Relations with Nurse Girl*' ran the *Weekly Dispatch*'s account of the divorce proceedings.) There were two sons, Graham and Colin, and a daughter who died in infancy. Husband number two was Captain George Thirkell, an Australian soldier who had contracted enteric fever after Gallipoli and, while on furlough in war-time London, was taken up by the Countess of Strathmore, whose daughter Lady Elizabeth Bowes-Lyon was shortly to marry the Duke of York the future King George VI.

There was another son, named Lance, more loyal than the first two – to the point of attempting to have his mother's no-nonsense *Oxford Dictionary of National Biography* entry bowdlerised – and an unfortunate removal to the groom's native Tasmania. Here, as Hall confirms, Angela was at out-of-place as a bird of paradise come to rest on the New Jersey turnpike. According to Graham, 'Broadly speaking Mother looked on Australians… as members of the Lower Classes.' On the other hand, she was consoled by a friendship with Dame Nellie Melba, and a ticket to the Government House Ball when the Yorks' Imperial tour brought them to Melbourne. There were also the beginnings of a literary career – newspaper articles, radio appearances and the draft of a first novel – even if the decision to pick up the pen could, in the light of Captain Thirkell's lack of earning power, be regarded as a fiscal necessity rather than a primal urge. 'We women' she wrote, around the time of the publication of her first novel, *Ankle Deep*, in 1933 'should be nothing but good to look at and restful to be with. But today's horrible economical conditions force us to be up and doing. No really nice woman ever ought to have to do *anything*.'

Irony, a constant presence in her novels, is conspicuously absent here. In teasing out the motives for her return (*sans* Captain Thirkell) to the Old Country, Hall prints a fascinating piece of reportage from Graham's memoirs:

> 'When are you coming back?' I said to the back of her head. She whirled on me this time, pushing the hair up out of her eyes.
>
> 'When your stepfather can earn some money to support us all!' she said with the teary edge to her voice that always intruded when she felt herself crossed. My stepfather, I thought? You mean your husband, don't you? But all I said was
>
> 'Are you taking the Sargent?'

Back in England, both before and after her abandonment of Thirkell, there were intriguing descents on the world of the Bright Young People (among other bright particular sparks of the London *beau monde*, she knew Rex Whistler and Stephen Tennant.) Meanwhile, a torrent of books had begun to stream forth from her fertile pen: two in 1933, three in 1934, another couple in 1935. For a supposedly reluctant author, her work-rate was dazzlingly, exhaustingly, unrepentantly prolific. The Royal Family were known to admire her – she received an invite to Princess Elizabeth's wedding in 1947 – and her popularity in the UK was soon replicated across the Atlantic: in July 1939 her British publisher, Jamie Hamilton, was able to assure her that with *The Brandons* she had fetched up on the American best-seller list. If there was one slight drawback to this comparatively sudden access of sales, money and celebrity, it comes in a comment from her son Colin: 'The whole of her writing years were those when she had ceased to love the world.'

* * * * * * * * *

Why should Angela have ceased to love the world? Marital troubles were part of it, naturally – one of the early novels is entitled *O, These Men, These Men!* Much more of it, though, is to do with a sneaking suspicion, repeatedly confirmed as the 1930s gave way to the 1940s, that Britain was becoming a much less hospitable place for Angela and her kind. Good on the associative network that sustained her subject's assaults on public life, Anne Hall seems rather less interested in her books, what they are about, and in particular the extreme conservatism that is, to a modern audience, their distinguishing mark. Wittily written, humorous, though with a more than occasional sombre edge, neatly constructed, often set in the imaginary English county of 'Barsetshire' (after Trollope) the novels are mostly about middle- to upper-middle-class people faced with the task of getting on or sometimes merely getting by in a world of high taxation, diminishing status, social insecurity and the triumph of Clement Attlee's Labour Government of 1945. 'What worries me' says one of her characters, 'is the deliberate extinction of the middle-class.' Another one of her spokespeople goes even further: 'When they have exterminated the middle-classes, England won't be any better.'

The choice of such a provocative verb – here in the post-Holocaust era, where cinema news reels offered nightly reminders of the horror of the death-camps – is quite deliberate. Camped out at her parents' house in Pembroke Gardens in the late 1940s, Angela liked to score through the headed notepaper brought from her previous address and replace it with 'Pembroke-Belsen Concentration Camp.' All this renders her a key, indeed an exceptional, figure in the all but unstoppable rise of the post-war right-wing English novel. One of the fascinations of the 1945–1960 era of British literary history is the conservatism that affects almost every level of literary production. If, at the top of the ladder, Evelyn Waugh and Anthony Powell were hard at work devising long novel sequences about the Second World War (Waugh's *Sword of Honour* trilogy, volumes seven to nine of

Powell's *A Dance to the Music of Time*) full of cunningly-wrought retrospective judgments about the idea of a 'People's War', then, down on the lower rungs, even the hedonistic jamboree that is H.E. Bates novels about the Larkin family turns out to be a covert attack on statism and interference.

Take, for example, Bates's *The Darling Buds of May* (1958) – not, the internal evidence suggests, set in the late 1950s but located nearly a decade before in bleak, ration-haunted 1949–50 when public enthusiasm for the Attlee project was in sharp decline. This surely explains the references to 'the National Elf lark' and talk of a judge forced to travel to a gymkhana by train as he cannot afford a car under 'this flipping government of ours.' Then there is modest Miss Pilchester, of whom Bates notes that before the war 'she had kept a little maid in the house, a man in the garden and a groom-cum-chauffeur-cum-cook… Now all of them are gone.' Beer-quaffing, roast goose-consuming, authority-loathing Pop Larkin is, we infer, just as much of a Tory as Angela's hard-pressed rural squires and shabby-genteel country solicitors wondering how they are going to educate their children. All that separates Thirkell man from Larkinland is a social divide and, it might be said, the sheer unmitigated virulence of the former's complaints.

In 'Towards the Cocktail Party: The conservation of post-war writing', his contribution to the symposium *Age of Austerity: 1945–1951* (1963), a youthful David Pryce-Jones suggests that in many ways Angela has the edge over Evelyn Waugh because of, rather than despite, 'her inferior style, literary quality and intellect.' Why? Well, according to Pryce-Jones, 'She recorded her version of the truth unadorned, and, far from crying *après moi le deluge*, she showed an intense fear of being sprinkled by any precipitate drops of rain.' For anyone wanting to understand how a substantial proportion of non-progressive, backward-gazing, middle-class British citizens felt about the post-war world and the people in charge of it, Thirkell's novels offer an invaluable cache of source material, if only because the sense of hurt, betrayal and contempt for the alien forces at work to disrupt national life is so unmediated. Even her blurb-writer, attempting to summarise *The Old Bank House* (1949), reckoned that 'The prevailing note is still kindliness… though it must be admitted that the note tends to tremble at the mention of "them"' – them being the Labour Party, whose defeat at the General Election of 1951 immediately produced a novel entitled *Happy Returns*.

As for that unmediated sense of hurt, here is a character from another of her titularly-signposted works, *Private Enterprise* (1947):

> What I really mind is their trying to bust up the *Empire*…
> I mean like leaving Egypt and trying to give Gibraltar to
> the natives. If they try to do anything to Gibraltar, I shall
> put on a striped petticoat and a muslin fichu and murder
> them all in their baths, because TRAITORS ought to be
> murdered.

Useless to contend that here is an imaginary person speaking in a work of fiction. This is Thirkell talking and she meant every word of it, from her lampooning of 'Kripps' (Sir Stafford Cripps, the deeply austere Labour Chancellor of the Exchequer) to a character named Captain Belton who ends a conversation by remarking that '"I daresay there is a Dictaphone behind the wainscot, and whoever is in charge of liquidating landowners taking it all down in shorthand.' Socialism, even of the English kind, meant a new type of authoritarianism that was possibly even worse than the brand that had been extinguished in the Second World War.

* * * * * * * * * *

Even die-hards acknowledged the increasing sourness of Angela's later output: as Elizabeth Bowen (a fan) noted, 'cantankerousness was to infect her work and chill her admirers.' In any case, there were other afflictions to worry her by this stage, existential threats that went far beyond designing Mr Attlee and his henchmen. They included declining health, aging parents to look after and, of course, the two elder sons, neither of whom she could get on with – several of their encounters carry a hint of actual violence – and whose own books she tended not to like. Colin, adding an extra vowel to his surname, became – as 'Colin MacInnes' – a considerable novelist in his own right; Angela reckoned him – this from a letter of 1952 – *'utterly unscrupulous… I would be quite happy never to see or hear from him again – but one's child is one's child, however odious.'* Many of the novels are still in print – several as Virago Modern Classics, which suggests that there is still an audience out there for the politically-charged middle-class, middle-brow fiction of seventy years ago. All the same, you suspect that she is the kind of writer whose real significance has begun to transfer itself into the field of social history. Not, of course, that there is anything unusual about this kind of disciplinary cross-over: exactly the same thing happened to Angus Wilson.

The New Criterion, 2022

DAVID LODGE: A QUESTION OF UPBRINGING

Quite a Good Time to be Born: A Memoir 1935–1975

One of the most tantalising fragments of David Lodge's jumbo-sized autobiography detaches itself from the wider stretch of the narrative on the day in 1959 when its hero, then aged 24, marries his long-term sweetheart Mary Jacob. Even by the standards of the 1950s it has been a protracted courtship – chaste, respectful, requiring frequent visits to the confession box and dating all the way back to the morning in September 1952 when the two newly-arrived undergraduates first set eyes on each other in the lino-carpeted administrative office of University College London's English Department. Triumphantly united with his bride, Burtons suit encasing his quivering flanks, Lodge, according to one critic of the wedding photographs, 'looked like the cat who had finally got the cream.'

And here the veteran Lodge-fancier will find memory tugging at his, or her, sleeve. Like Evelyn Waugh's Charles Ryder – a fictional exemplar several times invoked in the course of this groaning 500-page life-and-times – incredulously fetched up at a requisitioned, war-bound Brideshead, we have been here before. Intriguingly, as a glance at Lodge's sixth novel *How Far Can You Go?* (1980) rapidly confirms, more or less exactly the same description is applied to Dennis, the burly, acne-scarred, Eden-era Chemistry graduate stalled at the altar with his altogether scrumptious but long-resisting fiancée Angela. The latter, we are told, 'looked beautiful.' Dennis, on the other hand, resembled 'the cat who was finally certain of getting the cream.'

Just to complete the equation, *How Far Can You Go*'s subject matter is the progress, or otherwise, of a group of Catholic undergrads through the 1950s and on into the Age of Aquarius. Angela, as well as being skilled in the arts of natural childbirth, is also (like Mrs Lodge) the mother of a Down's Syndrome baby. Does this mean we can safely assume that Lodge is Dennis? In fact, this identification turns out to be the reddest of red herrings. Lodge, we soon learn, can be far more plausibly connected with 'Michael', a sex-fixated English student with a permanently bulging groin who writes a post-graduate thesis on Graham Greene (Lodge's own MA was entitled 'Catholic Fiction Since the Oxford Movement: Its Literary Form and Religious Content') and is described by his creator as 'a troubled character' who feels 'spiritually compromised by a habit of masturbation which he cannot kick and cannot bring himself to confess.'

Candour – real candour, that is, rather than Brand-style histrionics – is always an attractive quality in an autobiographer, and if this portrait of a furtive onanist slinking around the 'art-magazine' shops of the Charing Cross Road offers a new side to Professor David Lodge, M.A., PhD, novelist, screen-writer, proud author of *The Modes of Modern Writing* and much else high-grade critical work besides, then there are also some illuminating sidelights on how the fledgling writer and his wife – *The Picturegoers* (1960) was in the press by this stage – having 'got the hang of the basic act in the missionary position' by the time they returned from their honeymoon, gradually 'became less inhibited and more versatile lovers.'

Seen in its context – the 1950s and, worse than that, the *Catholic* 1950s – this is not quite funny, or as unintentionally funny, as it sounds. For one of *Quite a Good Time to be Born*'s principal themes, it soon transpires, is inhibition, how you overcome it, and the moral and practical consequences of that conquest, a sexual (and also a social and at times an intellectual) journey with, Lodge implies, many a consolation in store for the restricted once their shackles are finally hurled aside. There is, he reckons at the end of this affecting account of a Fifties courtship, much to be said for 'an unhurried exploration of the possibilities of erotic love, which may prevent desire from burning itself out early in a marriage and enable the enjoyment of physical intimacy to continue into old age.' At the same time he could probably have done without Catholic teaching on birth control, to which the Lodges zealously adhered until the mid-1960s.

Meanwhile, to go back to Dennis slavering at the altar, Lodge's *apologia pro vita sua* is brim-full of this kind of thing: authoritative little interventions in which Lodge hastens to assure us that while such and such an episode in one of his novels is taken entirely from the life, the reality drawn upon in another is – well I never – twisted irrevocably out of kilter. The ARP warden father in *Out of the Shelter* (1970), with its neatly evoked recollections of the Blitz, is not, in case you were wondering, Lodge senior (then somewhere in Scotland with the RAF) but an older man, while the short story 'When the Climate's Sultry', in which two holidaying Fifties couples stick to segregated rooms by night but pair off for afternoon siestas has consequences 'which should not be taken as biographical.'

If, on the one hand, *Quite a Good Time to be Born* is a rather straightforward, and at times downright pernickety, *résumé* of the way in which life transforms itself into art, then, on the other hand, the life undergoing this transformation is a fairly unusual one that, if only for socio-cultural reasons, deserves all the publicity it can get. After all, the 1950s – a decade in which Lodge passed his late teens and early twenties – were the age of what was known, even then, as the 'New Man.' And while the New Men came in varying shapes and sizes, from the nest-feathering technocrats of C.P. Snow and William Cooper's novels to the irony-wielding poets of the Movement and the existentialist horde urged into being by Colin Wilson's *The Outsider* (1956), Lodge himself is a highly representative specimen from their central strand: the upwardly-mobile grammar school boy from the lower-middle-class home, driven forward by educational opportunities that his parents could only dream of, lured into academe by the prospect of a degree and a superior white-collar job.

A good adjective for the family background would be 'Wellsian', which is to say suburban, cluttered – although Lodge himself was an only child – not too well-off and at times faintly mysterious. One grandfather was a Thameside publican. The other, 'Pop', had ne'er do well tendencies that left him faintly marginalised at clan gatherings. There was a buried artistic strain which made its way to the surface in the person of Lodge's father, William, an omnicompetent professional musician, who at one point featured in the house band at Mrs Meyrick's notorious Twenties speak-easy and Bright Young Person haunt the 'Forty-Three', in which Charles Ryder and Sebastian Flyte come to grief, and whose 'sweet tenor style' voice was only driven off the airwaves by the advent of American crooners.

Lodge is forensically astute about his upbringing in the dismal-sounding south-east London extremity of Brockley ('Brickley' in *The Picturegoers*), files a lengthy description of the cramped interior of 81 Millmark Grove, notes the peculiarity of a household routine geared to his father's being out every night and requiring silence every morning, and the consequent neglect of a mother who, as he puts it, was 'not sufficiently assertive to do anything about it.' A bright boy, whose life was not so much disrupted as offered a glimpse of new possibilities by the displacements of war, he sailed through the entrance exam to the local Catholic grammar school, would have sat his O Levels at 15 had the educational authorities allowed it (Lodge maintains that this proscription nurtured a lifelong distrust of bureaucracy), and, not without all parental misgiving, passed into UCL shortly before his eighteenth birthday.

Exposure to the vast secondary literature thrown up by the cultural end of the 1950s quite often encourages us to take the rise of the New Man for granted. Down in the lower reaches of the provincial university English department, at a time when 'English Studies' was only just being allowed a life of its own, the path to preferment could be surprisingly torturous. Kingsley Amis passed his pre-*Lucky Jim* years as an assistant lecturer at

Swansea in something very near poverty. The prodigiously well-qualified D.J. Enright, whose early criticism had appeared in *Scrutiny* when he was still an undergraduate, spent most of the period teaching abroad. Even Lodge, with his glowing first class degree and his well-notched academic bed-post, took the best part of a decade to establish himself: three years for a BA, two years National Service, two more years for an MA, a year at the British Council's London Overseas Student Centre, another year as a temporary assistant at Birmingham.

The army interludes, later worked up as *Ginger, You're Barmy* (1962), ram home Lodge's New Man credentials by placing him sideways-on to 'the Establishment', a phrase coined (by the journalist Henry Fairlie) at almost exactly the same time he set off for basic training at Bovington Camp in Dorset. As Jonathan Browne, his fictional alter-ego puts it – although Lodge offers his usual punctilious gloss on what did and didn't happen – 'I dimly perceived that I been wrenched out of a meritocracy, for success in which I was well qualified, and thrust into a small archaic world of privilege, for success in which I was singularly ill-endowed.' The un-noted connection here is with Simon Raven (b. 1927) whose essay 'Perish By The Sword', contributed to Hugh Thomas's symposium *The Establishment* (1959), though written by an ex-officer and gentleman rather than disaffected Lance-Corporal Lodge, makes similar complaints about what Raven calls 'a caste rooted in its own conception of superior, God-given status.'

The small world of privilege into which Lodge himself ultimately emerges turns out to be thoroughly up-to-date, or rather – an important distinction, given the paralytic slumber in which many post-war English faculties then reposed – in the process of becoming so. The University of Birmingham, whose English Department he permanently adorns from 1961 onward , is clearly his park and his pleasaunce, as Gerald Manley Hopkins said of Oxford, with Malcolm Bradbury shortly to arrive as his colleague and Richard Hoggart master-minding the nearby Cultural Studies centre. And if Lodge, in the context of his social and professional stamping-grounds, is a new kind of man then he and Bradbury are self-evidently a new kind of don – non-Oxbridge (Bradbury's path to Birmingham had taken him via Leicester, London, Manchester and Hull), keen on the latest evaluative trickery – Lodge's first critical work will be the formidably switched on *Language of Fiction* (1966) – but fascinated, if not absolutely seduced, by the world beyond the academic palisade, as likely to be found collaborating on revue sketches as conducting a graduate seminar, as happy to be occupied with a review for *Punch* or the *Tablet* – the old Catholic affiliations persist – as a commission from *Critical Quarterly*.

The faint air of self-consciousness that attends Lodge's account of his early dealings with media-land is something of a false trail, for it encourages the reader – the reader of literary autobiographies, anyway – to believe that he intends to take a theoretical interest in the kind of book he has written and the tradition in which it might be thought to repose. In the end, though, the genre into which *Quite a Good Year to be Born* very neatly slots – a fairly recent one, as it happens – doesn't seem to bother him. This is a pity, as Lodge's professional take on the subject of the middle-class literary memoir – as opposed to its distinguished forbear, the upper-class literary memoir – would be interesting to hear, for the differences that separate the two are quite as much a question of form as content and an area in which an emeritus professor of literature could have quite a lot of fun.

The key feature of the old-style upper-class English literary autobiography of the Anthony Powell/Michael Holroyd/James Lees-Milne type was a sense of self-deprecation amounting, at times, to outright concealment. No personal trumpets were ever blown; if pain was felt then it tended to be disguised as something else; and even professional jealousies came wrapped up in a kind of resolutely encrypted obliquity. The anguish that attended certain parts of Holroyd's *Basil Street Blues* (1999) is pretty much there for the reader to guess at: Holroyd might sometimes drop a hint or two, but inference is all. The middle-class literary autobiography is naturally much less discreet. If not exactly immodest, it is never shy of acknowledging its subject's successes, particularly as there is a social battle going alongside that gives the presence of a Lodge and a Bradbury *vis-a-vis* in Birmingham University's senior common room quite as much solidarity as Anthony Powell's understated accounts of the boys he messed with at Eton.

Even here in the stylised world of the middle-class literary memoir, though, there are distinctions to be drawn. The obvious parallel is with John Carey's *An Unexpected Professor* (2014), and yet it turns out to be unexpectedly far-flung. Each man is within a year of the other in age. Each was a grammar school boy from a London suburb. Each shares some of the experiences which middle-class men who got married and started having families in the twenty years after the war tend to have in common (both Lodge and Carey turn out to have been rapt spectators at the birth of one of their children.) But here the resemblances end, for Carey's book is shot through with a kind of personal myth-making that Lodge's attempt mostly avoids: the dragons of the Oxford senior common rooms there to be slain; the snubs from college grandees never forgotten, the vision of a university cleansed of its public school taint and filled with hundreds of embryo Careys never quite forgotten amid the tides of personal data.

Lodge, on the other hand, isn't much of a crusader, or a personal myth-maker, or even – notwithstanding the usual professional solidarity – an educationalist. Unlike Carey, a great proselytiser on behalf of grammar schools, he believes that the end of selective state education was probably a good thing. He distinguishing mark is simply his determination, a patient resolve to deal fairly with the world, look out for his own and his family's interests, enjoy the perquisites that come his way – such as the mid-60s American tour offered by his Harkness fellowship – and ensure that his very singular abilities aren't ignored either inside academe or beyond it.

Come this memoir's final lap, the question of Lodge's extra-academic career, and in particular the kind of novelist he imagines himself to be, is looming rather larger than before. As the middle sections of the book reveal in thorough-going detail, it was not enough for a Fifties-era writer to have merit: he, or she, had to fit in with the critical straight-jacketings of the day. The Pan paperback of *The Picturegoers* issued in 1962 bears a horribly close relationship to Alan Sillitoe's *Saturday Night and Sunday Morning* (1959), not least in the grimy realism of its frontispiece and the character CVs on the back ('MARK – who mapped out a girl's body and knew just how far she would let him go…' etc) But *The Picturegoers* is far too wry, far too spiritually absorbed, far too fond of pastiche-playfulness – a key Lodge attribute from the early days – to have its author marked down as an Angry Young Man.

So what kind of writer is he, as the Sixties gives way to the Seventies, as the Catholic church starts tentatively to accommodate itself to the modern world and the Lodges – their number now set at five – proceed on their meritocratic way? By this time informed observers are maintaining that the comedy of his third novel, *The British Museum is Falling Down* (1965), in which a Catholic postgrad and his wife try very hard not to have another baby, is preferable to the more realistic shadings of *Out of the Shelter*; critical reaction to the jet-setting academics of *Changing Places* (1975) bears them out (Bradbury's *The History Man*, another archetypal campus novel, is published in the same year.) We leave him marching on towards the sunlit uplands of professorships, best-sellers and TV work, and a literary world full of comfort and security for the people able to crack its code which, as he acknowledges in the preface, now seems as petrified as a dodo's egg. New Men, of course, become old men – a second volume is threatened – and 500 pages was possibly stretching it a bit, but as a piece of reportage from the third quarter of the English twentieth century this is a sociologist's paradise.

Guardian, 2015

IN SEARCH OF INEZ

INEZ HOLDEN – *There's No Story There:*
Wartime Writing, 1944–1945

Inez Holden's diary – a mammoth undertaking, only fragments of which have ever escaped into print – carries a rueful little entry from August 1948. 'I read *Brideshead Revisited* by Evelyn Waugh' the diarist writes. But the tale of Charles Ryder's dealings with the tantalising progeny of the Marquess of Marchmain, here in an unfallen world of Oxford quadrangles and stately pleasure domes, awakens a feeling of 'nostalgic depression.' This, she decides, is simply another of 'those stories of High Life of the Twenties which everyone seemed to have enjoyed but I never did.'

By this point in her career, Inez (possibly born in 1903, but more of this later) was a 20-year veteran of the London literary scene – and also of some of the more spangled redoubts beyond it. She starts turning up in magazine columns in the late 1920s: not as a writer but as an ornament of the hot-house enclosure stalked by the small group of party-goers and well-heeled socialites known as the Bright Young People. Evelyn Waugh's diary for May 1927, written when he was briefly attached to the *Daily Express*, mentions 'a charming girl called Inez Holden who works on the paper.'

The press photograph of the 'Impersonation Party', a legendary *Vile Bodies*-era rout in which each guest came as somebody else, depicts a throng of exotic cross-dressers. The Hon. Stephen Tennant masquerades as Queen Marie of Romania. Tallulah Bankhead, white-costumed with racket in hand, takes off the tennis player Jean Borotra. In the very middle of the tableau sits a small and inconspicuous girl in a Breton jersey. Of the celebrities stationed nearby, Elizabeth Ponsonby (the original of Waugh's Agatha Runcible) and Harold Acton are clearly having the time of their life, but Inez looks nervous, ill-at-ease, a rabbit caught in the flashbulb's intoxicating light.

The best memento of this phase of Holden's life is Anthony Powell's publishing caper *What's Become of Waring* (1939). Inez, her scope elaborated a little in the customary Powell manner, is Roberta Payne ('a tall girl with large black eyes which had a trick of increasing in area when she looked at you') a kind of book-world *femme fatale* who makes hay of the firm of Judkins and Judkins' timorous junior partner. As to how Roberta contrives to keep afloat on the listing late-Twenties tide, Powell's narrator writes only that 'she was usually so well housed and dressed that it was generally supposed that obscure rich men, too dull to be allowed to appear, contributed something to her upkeep.'

The young Holden, according to Powell's memoirs, 'lived fairly dangerously in a rich world of a distinctly older generation', a thin-ice skater, getting by on hand-outs, existing for the most part in shabby-genteel poverty Certainly, this is the milieu of *Born Old: Died Young* (1932), probably the best of her early novels, whose heroine is described as an 'adventuress', the daughter of an Edwardian beauty 'left homeless and penniless' and obliged to fend for herself. As a journalist, offering advice on such vital topics as 'Country House Bridge' to the readers of *Harpers*, she occupies a vantage-point that could have come straight out of Thackeray: an insider view that is sending up the social detail it imparts to amuse a readership that is simultaneously fascinated and repelled by the *recherché* information on offer.

If all this makes her sound like a cadet version of Nancy Mitford – no slouch herself at this kind of quasi-satirical journalism – then the reality of Inez's early life was a great deal starker. While the senior Holdens were *bona fide* Warwickshire gentry – her mother, Beatrice Paget, was reputed to be 'the second best woman rider in England' – they were so careless of their children's interests that Inez's birth went unregistered: the '1903' is guesswork. After a piecemeal education at a school for the offspring of poor tradespeople, where the fees were underwritten by a rich uncle, she escaped to Paris in her mid-teens and apparently never returned home.

By the time of *What's Become of Waring*, the landscapes of her rackety upbringing were far behind her. The partygoing had given way to radical socialism (Powell noted that 'her later passionate hatred of the Communist Party suggested close knowledge of its methods'), and the Bright Young People to friendships with H.G. Wells, whose lodger she briefly became, and a motley collection of war-era bohemians that included Stevie Smith and the Indian novelist Mulk Raj Anand. It was in her company that Powell and his wife Lady Violet, dining at the Café Royal in 1941, were first introduced to George Orwell.

The temptation of all this high-powered affiliation-brokering is to see Inez merely in the light cast by her more famous (and predominantly male) friends: the Orwell who 'pounced' on her at the end of an afternoon spent at Regent's Park Zoo (she was surprised by 'the intensity and urgency' of his attack) and who paid her to attend the films he was supposed to be reviewing for *Time and Tide* in his place; the Constant Lambert who appreciated her 'consumptive charm'; the Wells who while admiring her books, never forgave her for convening the quarrelsome dinner-party which produced a letter advising Orwell to 'read my early works you shit', and promptly evicted her from the mews flat in Hanover Terrace in revenge.

And yet Holden was perfectly capable of holding her own in this exalted company. Her contribution to 'Story by Five Authors' which Orwell commissioned for the BBC's Eastern Service during his time on its production staff is notable for containing a character who, as a posh upper-class type with bitter memories of his prep-school days and time spent serving in the Spanish Civil War, looks as if he were based on Orwell himself. Meanwhile, the fiction she was producing in the early 1940s, though framed in the decade's sharp, utilitarian light, set in factories, at town hall tribunals, in troop trains lumbering through the blacked-out English countryside, has a habit of transcending its origins and veering off into an imaginative space that most of the 1940s realists never penetrated.

There's No Story There, the latest Handheld Press reissue of her work (Kristin Bluemel's edition of *War Writing*, which combined her 1941 novel *Night Shift* with extracts from her diaries appeared in 2019), is a case in point. Set in 'Statevale', a gargantuan munitions complex in the middle of nowhere employing 30,000 workers and described as 'seven miles of carefully planned human paraphernalia', its techniques are those of the Mass Observation diarists. Just to reinforce this grounding in Holden's wartime job of touring factories to record their working conditions, one of the characters, the 'time and motion man' George Doran spends his leisure hours recording impressions of his fellow-labourers in his diary.

Sometimes Holden will pin one of her subjects down in a single sentence, as in the garrulous and supposedly 'schizophrenic' Ysabette, who insists that 'Almost all of my men friends are Group Captains.' On other occasions – mostly when she wants to make a wider point – she specialises in long, politically charged monologues. One worker, for example, praises Statevale's top-of-the-range facilities, while noting that 'It's very nice, of course, but it's taken a war to get it. They could have given us this all the time, then there wouldn't have been no trouble like there has been. And no war now, neither.'

Most of the novel's early chapters build up to its central set-piece: the arrival of a 'very distinguished personage', thought to be King George VI, at the site. But Holden's treatment of the Royal Visit is curiously, and, you infer, purposely, off-kilter – faithfully recording the wide-eyed chatter of the works canteen ('Mrs Bagaley saw King when he coom to Kindale, didn't you luv?'), but at the same time emphasizing the detachment of those onlookers for whom much more serious issues are at stake. Linnet, whose husband Willie is coming home that night on leave, absconds to a patch of nearby waste-ground nearby for a bunch of wild flowers to decorate the 'married quarters' in which she plans to entertain him. When someone asks her if she think 'he' will be wearing uniform, she assumes the question refers to Willie: 'Depends how much time he's got. Of course, he has to do what he's ordered.'

Predictably, the royal visit ends in anti-climax. 'King George' turns out to be pudding-faced, check-suited 'George King', a celebrated Lancashire comedian turned Hollywood film star with a nice line in homespun patter ('Of course, I've died plenty of times meself, but that wor' in pictures that wor'.') In her excellent introduction, Lucy Scholes suggests that by the end of World War II, 'Holden had transformed herself into a writer of documentary realism.' This is true, up to a point, but it is not the only thing that can be said of *There's No Story There*, which every so often cuts loose from its moorings in the tradition of war-time reportage and goes soaring off into flights of impressionist fancy. The girls in the canteen, for example, with their frothy Veronica Lake hair-dos and drumming high heels, 'gave the impression of a group of pretty centaurs handing out suppers in tune to hoof-sounds on kitchen tiles.'

Or there is her account of the security man Inspector Jameson hard at work interviewing a man named Lofty:

> The suit he wore was the same brown colour as the wood of
> the powerful bureau, so that Lofty had the impression that
> the Inspector's hands were severed from his body and he
> had simply unlocked one of the drawers in the desk, taken
> out a couple of hands and laid them down on the smooth
> brown surface of the bureau.

Elsewhere, the buses carrying early-morning workers to the site are said to come looming through the mist 'as purposeful as troop-carrying aircraft.' Orwell noted this tendency in her work, and a project to compile a volume of their war-time diaries was abandoned on the grounds of contending styles. As Bluemel notes in *George Orwell and the Radical Eccentrics* (2004), her account of the Holden-Smith-Anand nexus, he marked her journals down as 'feminine impressionistic.' Full of 'personal observations, character sketches and dialogues', her friend Celia Goodman remembered. 'Musical Chairman', 'Soldiers' Chorus' and 'Exiles in Conversation', three short pieces included in *There's No Story* pursue a similar line, full of painstaking reportage whose concentrated detail has the effect of turning them almost surreal, as if the characters had wandered off the set Holden has created for them to practise their lines in solitude.

Like many another writer who came to prominence during the war – Julian McLaren-Ross is an obvious example – Holden had trouble in sustaining a career beyond it. There were two more novels – *The Owner* (1952) and *The Adults* (1956) – but the bulk of her work in the 1950s consists of short stories commissioned by Powell in his capacity as literary editor of *Punch*. Her last years were spent in a flat in Lower Belgrave Square, where she died in 1976.

It would be wrong to over-state Holden's merits – she can be erratic, and one of the great drawbacks of documentary realism is its lack of narrative punch. On the other hand, 'Musical Chairman', which sees a young administrative assistant deputed to represent the Labour Exchange at the Local Appeal Board, is an extraordinary piece of work, full of bantering repartee ('Now that's a thing you don't often see?' 'What?' 'A lighter that lights') and indignant self-justification that manages to foreground the people uttering it like figures in a medieval frieze. Of all the under-sung women writers of the Forties – Monica Dickens, say, or Mollie Panter-Downes – coming to terms with new social arrangements and new ways of living, Inez Holden is the one who most needs to be revived, to see her short stories and her diaries in print, and a full-length biography devoted to her vivid yet infinitely mysterious life.

New Statesman, 2022

JOHN CAREY'S CLASS CONSCIOUSNESS

The Unexpected Professor: An Oxford Life in Books

One of John Carey's early predecessors in the Oxford Merton Chair of English Literature was Sir Walter Raleigh. Outwardly the connection between the two men is fairly slight. Raleigh (1860–1922) died in his early sixties, came to Oxford by a circuitous route that included a stint at the Mohammedan Anglo-Oriental College, Aligarth, and published very little during his time there. By comparison Professor Carey, still going strong in his eightieth year, has spent an entire academic life in sight of the Bodleian Library while writing, and compiling, enough books to fill a decent-sized shelf and enough literary journalism to put him in sight of his thousandth review. In the age of the media don, no modern academic, it might be said is quite so liberally bespattered with Grub Street mud.

And yet the links between the author of *Style* (1897), with its whimsical remarks about the teacher of writing's 'winged shoes' and the no-nonsense polemicist of *What Good are the Arts?* (2005) may be stronger than they seem. Both professors, it turns out, devoted a large part of their tenure to goading the shaky equipage of 'Oxford English' into some kind of forward motion. Each, more conspicuously, was remembered by their pupils as the most charismatic performer in the faculty (no college dining hall in the early 1980s was complete without someone trying an imitation of Carey's famous Dickens lectures.) Then, leaving all these minor similarities bruised and bleeding in the dust, there is the question of their very considerable asperity. Here, for example, we find Raleigh despatching a couple of picture postcards to a friend:

116

I send you Zola and Ibsen, an admirable pair... Look at them and think of Shakespeare's face, even in the Stratford bust. Or of Claverhouse's. Or of Robert Louis Stevenson's. Or of any decent midshipman. They both have bad mouths. I think we must frame them with the legend 'Modern Pigs' underneath. Myself I think their portraits an absolutely convincing and final criticism of their work: discussion is impossible after seeing them.

Compare this, a small matter of 70 years later, with the opening lines of Carey's review of *Children of the Sun* (1976), Martin Green's study of the English 'decadents' of the post-Great War era:

This book is richly stocked with people whom any person of decent instincts will find loathsome. That is partly what makes it fascinating, but also what makes it shaming, because the characters Martin Green describes dominated English cultural life from the end of the First World War until the fifties.

If part of the piece's interest lies in its blurring of the line between affrontedness and sheer effrontery, then the really fascinating thing about Carey on native decadence, or Carey on Evelyn Waugh, or Diana Mosley or half-a-dozen other of the subjects of *Original Copy* (1986), his bravura collection of occasional journalism, it is what lurks tantalisingly beneath: the suggestion of what Ian Hamilton, in reviewing Kingsley Amis's *Memoirs*, defined as 'a deeper enmity.' Carey's distaste for Brian Howard and Harold Acton, the twin leads of *Children of the Sun*, goes far beyond anything they may have written or said to the point where it becomes elemental, talismanic, an unignorable part of what might almost be called Carey's personal myth. The great merit of this entertaining memoir is its altogether remorseless exploration of the crucible in which a critical stance based pretty much on class consciousness came to be forged.

The Careys, their number amounting to six, with John the youngest child, were a quintessentially middle-class family from Barnes, London SW14, whom J.B. Priestley could have written about without peril to his conscience. Carey senior, much liked by his son, had been a prosperous accountant, but the firm went bust in the Depression and by the mid-1930s there was much less money to go round. Mementoes of bygone *luxe* occasionally floated to the surface: a black tail-coat; boxes of cigars; a white waistcoat hung in a wardrobe. There was also a curious older brother named Bill, who seems to have suffered from a kind of arrested development, if not autism, and of whose final years, when he came to stay in Oxford, on furlough from a psychiatric hospital, Carey will say only that 'these were not happy times.'

To these Balzacian shadings could be added an outsize helping of traditional English puritan purpose. A bright and studious teenager – though he is modest about his abilities – Carey duly proceeded to Richmond and East Sheen Grammar School for Boys, won a scholarship to St John's College, Oxford (his entry delayed by two years' national service in the East Surreys), took a congratulatory first, acquired a series of junior teaching posts and then, in his mid-twenties, was appointed a fellow of Keble, a college sunk in medieval torpor, where the rowing eight was restocked by a succession of dim-witted Etonians encouraged to read obscure and undemanding subjects such as the Diploma in Forestry.

By the time Carey and his wife Gill, met at an undergraduate lecture, are reinstalled in the much more luxurious purlieus of St John's – where they are provided with a proper house rather than a squalid flat over the warden's lodgings – *The Unexpected Professor*'s tripartite structure will have established itself in the reader's mind. About a third of it is that Powell-esque 'Question of Upbringing' (another writer who looms large in the Carey demonology.) Another third is reportage from the sensibility ladder, whose rungs led from *Chums* and *Tarka the Otter* to romantic poetry and, later on, the Milton studies on which his original reputation was based. The rest has to do with Oxford English, an institution that, while awarding degrees since the founding of the Merton Chair in 1885, seems scarcely to have developed in the first three quarters of a century of its existence. Unsurprisingly, the book is at its best, and also its funniest, when these three elements coalesce, when Carey's invincible sense of who is and where he comes from, not to mention the books he likes, collides head-on with an environment designed to call these affiliations sharply into question.

Even at officer cadet school, alas, the air is being made hideous by public schoolboys with names like 'Fitzherbert-Brockholes.' Inevitably, it is a great deal worse at Christchurch, for whose English tutor Carey fills in for a year in 1958–9, where even the buildings are 'an object lesson in how architecture can be used to make people feel small', the college staff enjoy being patronised by their blue-blooded charges and the distinguished economist Sir Roy Harrod declines to speak to him for the entirety of his appointment. Infuriated by the closed scholarship system which, as it seems to him, promotes mediocre public school talent at the expense of genuine live-wires from the grammar schools, Carey turns into an academic class warrior, encouraging sympathetic English masters to send him their best pupils. Meanwhile, as the English faculty, having shaken off the influence of Tolkien and C.S. Lewis, is being dragged, if not into the twentieth century then at least the latter stretches of the nineteenth, his own professional interests are following suit, from the pioneering study of Dickens's imagery (*The Violent Effigy*, 1973) to the equally ground-breaking *Thackeray: Prodigal Genius* (1977).

As for the asperity, well, this too is shaping up nicely. The Oxford English syllabus of the 1950s is 'a scandal or a joke, depending on your sense of humour.' *Don Quixote* is 'celebrated because virtually no one has read it.' *Idylls of the King* is an example of 'high Victorian bunkum.' The amusement to be gained from these irruptions of temperament is sharpened by the

119

ironies that run beneath, several of which Carey seems not to have noticed. At one point, for example, he ticks off the Matthew Arnold of *Culture and Anarchy* (the poetry is apparently 'undervalued') on the grounds that Arnold as a thinker is 'at best useless and at worst malign. Every thought that comes to him is drenched in the assumptions of his social class.' But could not the same, *mutatis mutandis*, be said of a critic who admits being drawn to the material that produced *The Intellectuals and the Masses* (1992) after coming across one or two of Virginia Woolf's more bracing remarks about the servant problem?

One of Carey's charms as a critic, it goes without saying, is his ability to have it both ways without seeming to notice that the trick is being played. Another is his prodigious self-confidence, the note that V.S. Pritchett caught (and admired) in Orwell's use of the word 'unquestionably' when making judgments that turned out to be all-too precarious. If there is a drawback to his class-consciousness, it lies in his reluctance to examine one or two of its implications, to concede that not all virtue is bred up in the greenhouses of the south-west London sprawl or even to allow that the idea of English social class is rarely as homogeneous, as innately cut-and-dried, as it seems. Carey's exceptionally astute biography of Golding [*William Golding: A Life*, 2009] falls half-way into this trap by contrasting Golding's time at Marlborough Grammar School, which left him with the feeling that he was 'not quite a gentleman', with the advantages of the posh public school down the road. True, no doubt, but the Old Marlburian John Betjeman was mocked on exactly the same grounds by his Oxford friends. Carey, you feel, has invested too much in Golding, chained himself too tightly to Golding's own mythological image, to be able to admit this relativism, and the best weapon for carving up the English social system is always a chopper.

If this *apologia pro vita mea* is rather light on relative values, then it is strong on sympathy, particularly for those whom Carey believes to have been conspired against or otherwise let down by institutions that ought to have protected them. One of its finest moments, for example, comes in a portrait of J.B. Leishman, the translator of Rilke, who preceded him at St John's, may have committed suicide and whom Carey thought sad ('I hope I am wrong about his being sad.') Did he, when it came down to it, actually enjoy his time in academe? Here the Walter Raleigh connection works again, for Raleigh was one of those anti-academics who, as John Gross once remarked, just happens to be an Oxford professor. In much the same way, Carey's famously debunking essay 'Down with Dons' (1974) could only have been written by a paid-up member of the cadre it affects to despise. On the other hand, to say that a number of different cakes are being had and eaten too in *The Unexpected Professor* is not to complain about their ingredients.

Times Literary Supplement, 2014

BRIAN SEWELL – *The Complete Outsider: Always Almost: Never Quite*

A fail-safe route into the combative life of the art-critic Brian Sewell (1931–2015) is by way of extended quotation. Here he is on the very first page of his voluminous memoirs, writing about the woman who brought him up:

> My earliest recollection of my mother is of my looking down on her and recognising fear. I have no memory of looking up at her, or seeing the bodyless head in which analysts who bother themselves with the earliest artistic impulses of the child would have us believe, the great smiling face of the adult looming over the cradle or the pram, but looking down from the not inconsiderable height of an overhanging branch has stayed with me all my life, not because of the adventure of climbing there – that I remember not at all – but for the startling clarity of a powerful emotion that I had never seen before and did not comprehend. The tree still stands in the garden of Cefin Bryntalch, an unlovely Victorian house in Powys recently described by agents selling it as 'innovative for its use of Neo-Georgian style which is worked into the expressive forms of brick vernacular revival' (house agents rival art critics in the meaningless jargon of their propaganda).

In the end there is something rather exhilarating about the sky-high levels of bitchiness on display in this carefully wrought charge-sheet, so much so that I began to make a list of the various people, artefacts, institutions and professions that Sewell is taking at pop at. There is his mother, obviously, and the 'fear' detected by her pint-sized, curly-haired son as he stares down at her, but a little investigation soon discloses at least five subsidiary targets. These include psychoanalysts (although the author of such a psychologically revealing book as *The Complete Outsider* might well have profited from a spell on the analyst's couch), realtors and art-critics, but also the unlovely house in which he spent his childhood. And then, most significantly of all, albeit only ticked off for juvenile incomprehension, there is Mr Sewell himself.

As a general rule, most memoirists with scores to settle tend to calm down as the years fly by: Mr Sewell isn't one of them. The wounds are still fresh and the bandages constantly renewed. To a roll-call of parents, realtors and unlovely Victorian houses can be added, before very long, the 'primped, perfumed and appalling' wives of his old school-friends, the distinguished artist Sir William Coldstream ('he had the mentality of a haberdashery assistant'), Sir Alec Martin of Christie's ('a formidable and ridiculous old fraud') and that grand panjandrum of the early twentieth-century art-world, Roger Fry, here stigmatised as 'the most pontifical, vainglorious, grandiloquent, superficial and, unfortunately, influential of all English art critics.' Naturally, this cavalcade of high-end disdain makes for a fascinating psychological puzzle. Is the spite and the fault-finding genuine – a kind of perpetual default setting – or is it done for effect, worked on and factitiously contrived, a part of the complex personal myth that one can see Sewell weaving around himself almost from the moment he was born?

The future art-world gadfly's origins were obscure, but, in the context of the semi-bohemian landscape he later came to occupy, by no means unpromising. He believed his father to be the musician Peter Heseltine/Warlock (1894–1930), who committed suicide six months before his putative son's birth. His mother, by contracting what later turned out to be a bigamous marriage to his stepfather in 1942, prompted his grandmother to make a new will 'in which no further provision of any kind was made for me. In effect I was wiped from the family' history.' The step-father's death left his second family penniless. It was a shabby-genteel, hand-to-mouth existence – Sewell suspects his mother of having worked as a prostitute – while not exactly lacking in exalted connections and fanciful redoubts. One of them was Madame Lipescu, mistress of King Carol of Romania, to whose Savoy Hotel suite Mrs Sewell was occasionally bidden (in later life, Brian was reminded of the whiffs of expensive perfume and body odour she gave off 'when required to squeeze the obstructed anal glands of a beloved bitch.') There was also, here in war-time London, a fair amount of danger, exemplified by the summer day on which, hand-in-hand in Kensington High Street, mother and son were blown by a bomb-blast through the window of a nearby shop.

The accompanying photographs testify to what an odd little chap – to use the English vernacular of the time – young Brian must have been. Aged three, clad in buttoned top-coat with velvet collar, he looks like Christopher Robin with a perm. Aged 16, several inches shorter than any of his team-mates, hair sprouting off the top of his head like a furze-bush, he stands in the back-row of a school rugby team, like some changeling dropped out of the clouds. The school was Haberdasher's Aske's, in north-west London, about which he complains ('I hated most of my schoolmasters'), but whose teaching was sufficiently adept to gain him a place at Oxford. This, as a precocious teenage *habitué* of the London sale rooms, already prone to spending his pocket-money on three guinea bundles of uncatalogued drawings, he naturally turned down in favour of the Courtauld Institute Here he was taken up by Anthony Blunt, authority on Poussin and Keeper of the Queen's Pictures – on a trip to Windsor with his patron, Sewell finds himself perched on a ladder when Her Majesty enters the room – and sent forth on the proper business of his life.

Even at this stage, you can see why Sewell – petulant, fastidious and oozing wounded *amour propre* – got on so badly with so many of the people he rubbed up against. What redeems this catalogue of put-downs and airy condemnation, alternatively, is the sheer unpredictability of the persona on display. There are times when all the gadding about, the name-dropping and the epithet-flinging threaten to turn him into a type. More often, though, Sewell is like the character in the high-class novel who delights in confounding the reader's expectation of him, and reinforces the solidity of his role by every so often stepping out of it. The two years' compulsory military service that most Fifties-era young British men regarded as a waste of time offers him the chance to learn practical skills and hone his 'ruthlessness.' The homosexual leanings he had detected at Haberdasher's Aske's ('I was, I am certain, already queer at school') were countered by a piety that led him to think seriously about becoming a Catholic priest. And then there is his sense of humour – waspish and vengeful, certainly, but also capable of realising great comic moments. Thus, while attending an officer's training course, and ordered to address the assembled recruits, he opts to lecture on the absence of sexual imagery from pre-Colombian Mexican sculpture. 'I can't help feeling I've had my leg pulled' the supervising officer remarks, 'but it makes a change from how to look after a horse.'

Even the name-dropping is of a somewhat specialised kind, in which the lustre and *éclat* is not so much recognised as semaphored at with what will very often reveal itself as faint disparagement – of the great post-war triumvirate of Francis Bacon, Lucian Freud and David Hockney, for example, he remarks only that he knew them 'long before I took to criticism and it never occurred to me that every word they uttered should be preserved by some devoted amanuensis.' Christie's, the great London auction house, to which he eventually proceeded, might have seemed a natural milieu in which these talents – if that is what they were – could be exercised, but as ever Sewell is pulled both ways, relishing his imbrication in the business of identifying, talking up and selling art, but disillusioned by the gargantuan helpings of prejudice and snobbery on display: 'We've already got one homosexual on the board' some grand eminence declares when there is talk of giving him a directorship. In fact, the atmosphere at King Street, St James, Christie's London HQ is practically Firbankian in its shadings – a world of chilly cruelty and archaic protocols irradiated by a procession of Dickensian grotesques.

Most 600 page autobiographies (this one combines two volume previously published in 2011 and 2012 as *Outsider I* and *Outsider II)* eventually run out of steam before the ship sails home to port. *The Complete Outsider*, so fascinating in its world-within-a-world account of London gay life in the pre-Wolfenden days, so lyrical when art history is brought to bear on its figurative language (see the description of black GIs lying in wait for factory girls as 'wicked stuff for Burra watercolours'), is just slightly less absorbing once Sewell has said goodbye to Christie's, embarked on a career as a private dealer and settled down – not really the *mot juste*, given the rebarbativeness of what got written by and about him – as art critic of the *London Evening Standard*. It is not that Sewell's sense of humour deserts him – when sheltering the disgraced Blunt after the latter's exposure as a Russian spy (at some personal cost) and trailed by the media he regrets that he can no longer call in at Harrod's Knightsbridge department store in search of a casual pick-up in the washroom. It is merely that by his last couple of decades he has become one of those omnipresent sub-celebrities known in the UK as a National Treasure. Again, the question of motivation rears its head. Did the art critic who so violently repudiated Damien Hirst, who criticised Hockney's vulgarity, who maintained that there has never been a first-rate woman artist and of whom dozens of people wrote to his editor to protest that he was 'homophobic', 'misogynistic' and 'elitist', really believe his pronouncements, or was he just having a little fun?

On the other hand, as very often happens with the flamboyantly opinionated, it may simply be that the stylisation of one's personality required by this kind of attitude is such that manner, stance and judgment are ultimately inseparable from each other, and that the pundit who volunteered such glacial observations on great works of art was in danger of becoming one himself. All this leads to a further question, posed by the book's title. One should always be suspicious of people who make claims to outsider status, if only because it usually takes an insider to be in a position to make them. A genuine British outsider, you feel, would be someone like James Thompson the younger (1834–1882), semi-impoverished author of *The City of Dreadful Night* (1874), whose existence on the margins of the cultural world of his day is symbolised by the story of his trudging through the rain to watch George Eliot's funeral, only to have his view obscured by the forest of lofted umbrellas. Gay, illegitimate, lower-middle-class and the practised expounder of unfashionable views Brian Sewell may have been, but he also won a place at a major British university, studied at the Courtauld, hobnobbed with Anthony Blunt, wrote art criticism for a leading newspaper and made television programmes for the BBC. This is not to minimise the importance of the personal myth, or its role in making the average life tolerable, and without the view of his path through life that he took Sewell would not have been the person he was. All the same, large parts of his career may be regarded as an object lesson in how to worm your way into the heart of the crowd.

The New Criterion, 2020

EDWARD CHANEY – *Genius Friend: G.B. Edwards &*
The Book of Ebenezer Le Page

The Book of Ebenezer Le Page, Gerald Edwards's only full-length
work, was originally published in 1981 to reviews that bordered
on the ecstatic. William Golding declared that to read it was 'not
like reading, but living.' John Fowles, charmed by its Guernsey
patois and worm's eye view of 70 years or so of Channel Island
history, suggested that voice and method were so unusual 'that it
belongs nowhere on our conventional literary maps.' Its author,
by this stage, was five years dead, leaving publication to be
contrived by his much younger friend, a PhD student named
Edward Chaney, now risen to the Professorship of Fine and
Decorative Arts at Southampton Solent University.

It would be wrong to call *Genius Friend* – a description coined
by Edwards's one-time ally John Stewart Collis – a biography, for
it is both something more, and at times something rather less,
than a straightforward chronological narrative. Several of the later
chapters – these have titles like 'Rejected by Cape' and 'Approach
to Faber' – are given over to Professor Chaney's dealings with the
countless publishers who turned his hero's masterpiece down.
Other reproduce Edwards's appreciative but, at times, queerly
cantankerous late-period letters. The first half of the book, on the
other hand, is a much more conventionally framed attempt to
map out one or two of the circles in which Edwards moved
during his brief early 1930s heyday.

Not that 'heyday' is the right word for the fathomlessly
obscure existence that Edwards (1899–1976) pursued at this, and
indeed most other times. The difficulty in writing about him, as

Chaney acknowledges, lies in how little is known about him and how resolutely this practised letter-burner and early work-destroyer succeeded in covering up his tracks. Take away typescript and printed version of *Ebenezer* and the bibliography of his writings is reduced to precisely 14 items. The life, too, is full of utterly un-navigable terrain, to the point where in the post-1950 period, when thought to be working as a civil servant, Edwards disappears entirely from the societal map. All that is known of his 1960s wanderings, for example, is that he 'lived rough' for a while in Wales before consecutive three-year stints in Penzance and Plymouth

All the evidence – not that there is very much of that – suggests that Edwards rather enjoyed this deliberate obfuscation, and that the faint air of mystique that surrounded both present and past life was important to him. 'The mere thought of having a public image appals me' he told Chaney late in life. 'I would not willingly supply the public with any autobiographical data whatever.' All that is really known of his early career is that he was born on the island of Guernsey, spent the years between 1919 and 1923 at the University of Bristol (subjects and degree unknown) migrated to London, married a woman named Kathleen Smith, by whom he had two children, and combined lecturing for Toynbee Hall and the Workers' Educational Association with a little – a very little – highbrow journalism for the *Adelphi*, then edited by John Middleton Murry.

Perhaps, in the end, this recitation tells us more about Edwards than he would have wanted us to know, for it locates him in that marginal but curiously enticing quadrant of the late Twenties literary world populated by high-minded and sexually liberated experimentalists who had mislaid God in Shaw and found him again in Lawrence while never quite disdaining the pull of likely-sounding theosophists such as Annie Besant, who rates half-a-dozen index references – against Nietzsche's 23, that is,. The quarterly *Adelph*i, to which the young Eric Blair contributed at exactly the same time as Edwards, at least once in the same issue, turns up in his alter ego George Orwell's *Keep The Aspidistra Flying* (1936), lightly disguised as *Antichrist*, 'a middle- to highbrow monthly, Socialist in a vehement but ill-defined way' of which it is said that 'it gave the impression of being edited by an ardent Nonconformist who had transferred his allegiance from God to Marx, and in doing so had got mixed up with a gang of *vers libre* poets.'

If Edwards's all too brief association with the *Adelphi*, his Shavian fixations (Shaw, he decided, had 'betrayed courage'), and his friendships with contemporaries such as Collis and Stephen Potter (the future author of *Gamesmanship* but then a very serious young Lawrentian) offers a context for his rackety early years, then so does the tiny amount of information that survives about his personal life. His marriage to what a friend called 'the least monogamous woman I have ever known' had broken down by the mid-1930s, preceded by several stays in 'experimental communities' both at home and abroad and a trip in search of Lawrence, who died before the two could meet. Come 1939, children abandoned to foster-care, he was working for Mass Observation in Bolton, where a colleague remembered him as '*very* intelligent... *very* temperamental' and apparently homosexual.

The Bolton job for Charles Madge and Tom Harrison's team also involved the production and the acting in of plays for the local Drama School. Thereafter the creative curtain dropped and whatever work Edwards was engaged in until the early 1970s, when, in the relative comfort of a Weymouth lodging house, he began to write *Ebeneze*r, no longer survives. There are several questions to be asked of these long years of self-sequestration, but the obvious one is that of professional *nous*. Why, to put it starkly, was the protégé of Middleton Murry, the man unquestionably accepted as a 'genius' by his friends – Potter remembered displaying a copy of the Shaw essay to Collis with the words 'I am absolutely certain that some day this will be worth quite a lot of money' – unable, or perhaps only unwilling, to make a success of literary life?

One answer, which even Professor Chaney tactfully allow, is his cheery procrastinating. The Lawrence book was never completed, and the letters home to Murry mingle requests for another 20 francs with excuses for unfinished tasks that sometimes seem to betray an odd self-satisfaction ('The fact that I didn't manage to get anything to you for this quarter's *Adelphi* is something I don't like to think about. I am inexcusably to blame – and yet not to blame at all…') Much more damaging to his prospects, you feel, was the loftiness of tone that distinguished his sporadic appearances in print, sometimes descending into outright hectoring. Potter, who wrote the study of Lawrence that his friend had only contemplated, was briskly informed that 'this book seems to me as bad a book as a book on Lawrence could be. And why is it bad? Because it is utterly heartless.'

The spikiness kept up: even in his last days, in what seems to have been the congenial environment of Mrs Snell's lodging house, he once strode so dramatically from a room in which he had lost his temper that the door handle remained in his hand. Curiously, little of this tension, the sense of inner fires steeply banked that hangs over his practised disinclination to review Murry's *God, being an Introduction to the Science of Metabiology* even when the rent wants paying, extends to *The Book of Ebenezer Le Page*. Certainly Edwards appears in it, but only as the character Raymond Martel, and Ebenezer himself is not a highbrow from a Garsington lawn trying to work out what he thinks of the path to Godhead but a Guernseyman bred up on whimsy and tomatoes, the smell of the sea and his intense dislike of Jersey.

Perhaps, in the last resort, Edwards could only achieve the kind of aesthetic effects he sought by detaching himself from the creative process, by fashioning a medium in which, so to speak, he is not playing all the parts himself *Ebenezer*, after all, garrulous, dense and elegiac, is an exercise in ventriloquism. The real subject of the early essays, you feel, whether written to impress or to annoy, is their self-consciousness, the author's growing awareness of the kind of person he is, an acute sensitivity to criticism that tends to manifest itself in the pre-emptive strike. There is a rather revealing letter to Murry from 1929, *apropos* an unpublished work entitled *Margaret*, which insists that 'Your criticism of my play delighted me. Of course you are substantially right – though you're too good to me on the way it's done: but then I can see its patches, and I have my own tricks and wickedness.'

There is a calculated *sang-froid* about this, a suspicion that Edwards doesn't really care about Murry's criticism, that the real delight lies in the tricks and wickedness. *Genius Friend*, meanwhile, is a consistently fascinating work while – almost inevitably, given the dearth of source material – digressive to the point of mania. When not luxuriating in half-page disquisitions about 'unjustly forgotten' philosophers in whom Edwards may have taken a passing interest, reading the four-page extract from *Twilight in Italy* that Chaney shoehorns into his account of a trip to Switzerland, the reader may pause to admire some song lyrics penned by the author's daughter Olivia or wonder why the footnote about Edward Heath, for whom Edwards admits to not having voted in 1974, should contain the information that he was one of only four unmarried Prime Ministers.

For the most part, Chaney's commendable attempts to 'place' his subject are confined to the very limited inter-war cultural landscape in which he operated, although there are suggestive comparisons to Lampedusa.. But in some ways his cultivated detachment from the mainstream belongs to an older literary world. There is an authentic existential bitterness, to borrow John Gross's phrase, about some of his pronouncements which puts you mind of Victorian models – James Thomson the Younger, say – and an individuality of stance which renders the period yardsticks against which he might be measured largely irrelevant. What remains are the leavings of a genuine literary outsider, whom no amount of sanctification can ever quite dislodge from his self-manufactured niche.

Times Literary Supplement, 2016

IV. ANNIVERSARIES

NINETEEN SIXTY-SIX AND ALL THAT

More than one British writer was at least indirectly implicated in the events of 30 July 1966. Gordon Williams, whose *From Scenes Like These* (1968) went on to be short-listed for the very first Booker Prize, found himself commissioned to ghost-write the England captain Bobby Moore's press columns and assemble his best-selling autobiography *My Soccer Story* (for the record, Williams remembered his employer as table-bestriding, trouser-lowering 'raucous Bobby', quite unlike the sober Corinthian offered up for public consumption.) Yet pride of place in the pantheon of late Sixties soccerati – a term not coined for another quarter of a century – must surely go to the avant-garde novelist and one-time *Observer* football correspondent B.S. Johnson.

As early as November 1965, the author of *Travelling People* was hired by the Chilean movie producer Octavio Senoret to write the script of a FIFA-sponsored cinema film of the tournament. The aim, Johnson breezily declared in a magazine interview, was to 'make something even better than the Japs did of the Tokyo Olympiad.' He produced an idiosyncratic text, much concerned with the buildings of central London and name-checking his two current heroes, the brutalist architects Peter and Alison Smithson, and was duly sacked from the project on 19 July. Undeterred by this rebuff, Johnson filed a report on the game for the *Times of India*, a bravura piece acclaiming a match that 'must surely stand with the greatest ever played, a match that had as many changes of fortune and direction of a gypsy's life...' There was even an unpublished poem entitled *World Cup Shot*:

> I must have seen it forty times:
> Taking the ball past one, another,

Stumbling, recovering, scoring
Always I wanted the defeated full back
To stop him
Ah, the chances let slip!

To judge from the fragment of unused screenplay printed in Jonathan Coe's biography (*Like a Fiery Elephant: The Story of B.S. Johnson*, 2004), with its wide-angle shots of fathers teaching their sons to dribble, kick-abouts in school playgrounds and Carnaby Street shop-windows, Johnson seriously believed in the idea of football as a unifying force, capable of forging bonds between parents and their children and transcending the barriers of class and geography. One or two of the ornaments of Harold Wilson's recently re-elected Labour government clearly thought the same. 'A tremendous help for him [Wilson] that we won the World Cup on Saturday', the Secretary of State for Housing. R.H.S. Crossman, wrote in his diary on 31 July, going on to add that it 'could be a decisive factor in strengthening sterling…'

The mythological significance of World Cup year, the suspicion that the 12-month period between January and December 1966 represents a kind of gigantic metaphorical tipping-point, extends to vast areas of our national life. If it was the year in which Alf Ramsay's doughty gladiators 'brought football home' once more to the country of its birth, while contriving to win a figurative Third World War against their cup-final opponents West Germany along the way, then it was also a year in which Labour claimed its biggest electoral victory since the Attlee landslide of 1945. Popular music, too, as Jon Savage reminds us in his recent *1966: The Year the Decade Exploded*, was tantalisingly poised between the beat group explosion of 1963–5, mod cacophonies and the psychedelic wig-outs inaugurated by the Beatles' *Sgt Pepper's Lonely Hearts Club Band* in the early summer of 1967.

Not, of course, that many of these trails led anywhere in particular. Ramsay's heroes may have reached the quarter-final of the next World Cup in Brazil four years later, but they failed even to qualify for the 1974 tournament. The Wilson government emerged from an economic crisis and a Chancellor's resignation to plunge itself into a bruising stand-off with its trades union backers over 'In Place of Strife'; over on the opposition benches, 'Selsdon Man' was already making his presence felt among the Tory think-tanks. And in the hot-house conditions of the mid-Sixties tin pan alley, according to the late Ian Macdonald's *Revolution in the Head: The Beatles' Music and the Sixties*, lay the seeds of popular music's decline: after *Sgt Pepper*, it could be argued, came self-indulgence, bombast, heavy metal thunder. Meanwhile, as a phenomenon 'the Sixties' go on being mythologised and misinterpreted, and – it might be argued – having more significance extracted from them than they can decently stand.

How was the decade exploding, or otherwise, over in the world of literature? Books, as John Gross once pointed out, rarely fit into this kind of conceptual straight-jacket. Periods bleed into one another; gnarled veterans of a bygone age survive to buck the prevailing trend. At first glance, the literary world of 1966 offers only a bewildering variety of styles. It was an age of self-conscious avant-garderie, and also an age of carrying on as usual. It was the year of J.G. Ballard's *The Crystal World* and the year of Nancy Mitford's *The Sun King*, the year of Anthony Powell's *The Soldier's Art* – the eighth instalment of a novel sequence running back to 1951 – and Christine Brooke Rose's determinedly elliptical *Between*. It was the year in which Evelyn Waugh died and Sarah Waters was born, the year of Susan Sontag's *Against Interpretation* and Jean Rhys' *Wide Sargasso Sea*, of Basil Bunting's *Briggflatts* and Kingsley Amis's *The Anti-Death League*. Modernists and mad-lads jostle Thirties mandarins and one-time Angry Young Men, in a landscape whose major contested event was the defeat of Robert Lowell by Edmund Blunden – a convincing 477 votes to 241 – in the Oxford Professorship of Poetry election.

Blunden's supporters included Philip Larkin, who explained to his friend Robert Conquest that 'I didn't, of course, vote, but if I had I'd have voted for Blunden – who was a faint amount of good once – not like old R.L., who's never looked like being a single iota of good in all his born days.' Blunden had been born as long ago as 1896, and one of the most striking aspects of a world otherwise awash with poetry 'happenings' Merseyside patois and English Beats, is the presence in it of large numbers of writers whose careers had begun before the Great War. T.S. Eliot had died the previous year, but E.M. Forster, Siegfried Sassoon, Ivy Compton-Burnett, Osbert and Sacheverell Sitwell and Frank Swinnerton were still going strong. Sir John Masefield (born in 1878) continued to officiate as Poet Laureate – a post to which he had been appointed as long ago as 1930 – and there were new works by the 85 year-old P.G. Wodehouse and the 83 year-old Compton Mackenzie to compete with the first novels of Angela Carter and Eva Figes.

The same air of continuity could be felt on the books pages, where for all the recent arrival in Grub Street of no-nonsense newcomers such as Karl Miller and Brigid Brophy readers of the *Sunday Times* could still admire the gentlemanly encomia of the Bloomsbury veteran Raymond Mortimer born 1895) and Cyril Connolly (born 1903). To read the diaries and letters of the period is to marvel at how familiar, if not sempiternal, are most of the complaints. John Fowles reports from America the feeling, common to nearly every literary decade, that the novel is a condemned form, has a few decades more of life and then will disappear' before going on to castigate the 'sick culture' of which he was a part and declare that 'the English reader is dead.' Philip Larkin, meantime, was lamenting the over-exposure of certain of his remorselessly productive peers. 'The whole of English Lit. at the moment is being written by Anthony Burgess' he informed Anthony Thwaite. 'He reviews all the new books except those written by himself... He must be a kind of Batman of contemporary letters.'

Elsewhere, the scapegoat was age-old writerly flamboyance,

with Angus Wilson writing home to his partner Tony Garnett from a tour of Australia to protest at the arrival in his hotel room of Yevgeny Yevtushenko 'with a blonde pick-up (a nice Australian girl) and waking me so that I shouted but being awfully nice with a bottle of champagne at 4 in the morning.' Many of the year's great literary *cause célèbres*, it turns out, were determinedly backward-looking. Frances Partridge's diary for 1966 records time spent poring over the manuscript of Michael Holroyd's forthcoming life of Lytton Strachey (Mrs Partridge feared that Holroyd had underestimated the 'nobility' of the old Bloomsburians, while allowing that 'they were also of course a little absurd') and there was a corking row over Beverley Nichols's *A Case of Human Bondage*, a somewhat partial defence of Somerset Maugham's wife Syrie, deplored by Noel Coward, who featured in it, as 'vulgar, tasteless and inaccurate.'

From the angle of the mid-60s talent pool, this backward gaze is thoroughly excusable. Many of the decade's writers, now moving into their fifties and sixties, were still busily unpacking semi-autobiographical baggage from twenty or even thirty years ago. *The Soldier's Art*, the second of Powell's three war novels, covers the early part of 1941. William Cooper's *Memoirs of a New Man* has a contemporary setting, but the archetype canvassed by the title is C.P. Snow's upwardly mobile inter-war era grammar school boy, zealously at large in Whitehall's corridors of power. Even a comparative youngster like the 39 year-old Simon Raven could be found devoting large parts of *The Sabre Squadron*, the third volume in his *Alms for Oblivion* sequence, to recollections of his army days in the Occupied Germany of the early 1950s. Offered a lift in a superior's official car, Cooper's civil servant hero Jim Carteret notes that it was 'commodious in the style of an earlier period.' So were a good many items proudly displayed on the Class of 1966 fiction shelf, from Iris Murdoch's *The Time of the Angels* to Robert Liddell's *An Object for a Walk*.

If there was a generational divide, it became sharply apparent in the mid-60s hankering for 'experiment', a self-conscious determination to steer the novel even further along channels first mapped out by Joyce and Beckett. 'I was young enough to believe that I and a few other writers with similar ideas would change the face of English fiction' Eva Figes later remarked of her debut novel. Critical responses to such fictions as Figes' *Equinox*, a study of the mind of a woman whose marriage is breaking down, Johnson's *Trawl*, a densely modulated account of a fortnight spent on a North Sea trawler, and Maureen Duffy's *Microcosm*, a pioneering take on the then hidden world of London lesbianism, occasionally extended to discussions of the 'anti-novel', a gleeful perversion of traditional forms in which plot, cohesion and character – what Martin Amis once called the 'staid satisfactions' – were elbowed aside by non-linear narratives, streams of consciousness, syntactical free-for-alls and serial fragmentation.

The 'anti-novel' gets several approving mentions in Sebastian Groes' nicely provocative *British Fictions of the Sixties: The Making of the Swinging Decade* (Bloomsbury Academic, 2016.) Groes' thesis – not, it should be said, entirely original – is that people who wish to understand the 1960s have essentially been reading the wrong books, sticking to drab works of realism when the key to the era's significance lies in spikier and more left-field correctives. His aim, as he puts it, is 'to challenge the existence of a straightforward causal correlation between socio-historical context and artistic representation.' To him the Sixties are 'a revolution of the mind', an acceleration of that much bruited post-Enlightenment 'crisis in meaning' and – in another version of the tipping-point theory previously applied to football, politics and pop – 'an epistemological hinge moment that is clothed in myths implicated in shaping our understanding of the past, our present moment and the future of our twenty-first century world.'

And I like B.S. Johnson too, although it is difficult to imagine that his notoriously self-absorbed and curiously naïve approach to novel-writing – that standard Sixties line about reality only being navigible through the doorway of your own partial consciousness

– represents much in the way of an epistemological hinge moment. The drawback of Groes' approach is that for all its much-vaunted pluralism, the fault-lines between the writers he does (and doesn't) mention are far more strictly demarcated than they were at the time, that – to put it starkly – one critic's mainstream traditionalist is another's avant-garde outlier. You would never guess from him that Johnson was sometimes regarded as a realist of the old school whose proudly-borne special effects were seen as more of a hindrance than a help, or that the distinguishing mark of *The Soldier's Art* is its playfulness, a ludic quality that is never so apparent as in the opening scene in which Nick Jenkins, buying an army greatcoat in a shop that also sells theatrical costumes, is mistaken by the assistant for an actor.

For Powell the dialogue exchanges that follow ('What's this one for?' 'Just the war.' 'I'll bear the show in mind') are not an incidental garnish, but something integral to his idea of the ominous yet undeniably aesthetic spectacle of which armed conflict consists. Leaving the shop, he finds himself developing the metaphor: 'Now that the curtain had gone up once more on this old favourite – *The War* – in which, so it appeared, I had been cast for a walk-on part, what days were left before joining my unit would be required for dress rehearsal. Cues must not be missed.' The cues missed by most of the Sixties avant-garde, on the other hand, were those of straightforward narrative satisfaction. No doubt there is a certain amount of historical curiosity to be slaked by re-reading a novel like *Trawl* half a century after it was written, but that is where most readers' interest will stop. We – or most of us – read Johnson, and Alan Burns and Ann Quin to see what clever young literary people were up to in the era of Flower Power, Vietnam and Mary Quant, not in the way that we read Dickens, or Thackeray or even Anthony Powell.

Then there is that vital question of milieu, an area that Groes himself, with his talk of preponderant myths and his sub-title about the 'swinging Sixties', seems to have his doubts about. If the Sixties offered a 'revolution of the mind', then where exactly, other than in the mind itself, was that revolution taking place? According to the social historian David Kynaston – now up to 1962 in his multi-volume history of post-war Britain – the 1960s, as represented by posthumous media commemoration, really only happened in a few square miles of central London. The rest of the UK barely noticed they had gone by. Naturally, zeitgeist works in mysterious – and multifarious – ways: one can be influenced by The Beatles without actually having heard any of their music; and one can be suffering from an existential crisis without knowing that such things as existential crises exist. At the same time, it is perfectly possible that a novel by, say, A.J. Cronin will offer just as much of a conduit into ordinary people's heads as one by J.G. Ballard.

All the same, it would be wrong to pretend that the experimental virus hadn't penetrated deep into the bloodstream of mainstream English fiction, or that the range of stylistic tics and behavioural preoccupations it brought with it aren't immediately visible in dozens of the period's best-known novels. Piers Paul Read, for example, was soon to establish himself as a Catholic realist – if that is not an oxymoron – but his 1966 debut, *Game in Heaven with Tussy Marx*, is a much more oblique work, in which a band of celestial observers sits chatting blithely about the meaning of existence while a corrupt and anarchic world boils away beneath them. The same point can be made of the year's top-ranking literary bestseller. Set on a Greek island, and featuring a nihilistic young man given the run-around by a manipulative mage-figure, John Fowles's *The Magus* wears its Sixties preoccupations (Freud, Jung, *animas*) like so many war medals.

The Magus, Fowles tells us in his preface to the sexed-up revised edition of 1977, was very nearly called *The Godgame*: certainly there are moments when what begins life as a study in existentialism gradually begins to mutate into a kind of existential burlesque. But Nicholas d'Urfe's ordeal on 'Phraxos' (in reality Spetnai, where Fowles had taught in the early 1950s) has its retrospective side. The island is haunted by memories of the Nazi occupation. Conchis, his tormentor, may or may not have been a collaborator. And forever lurking in the background is the phantom of an older England – the world inhabited by Nicholas's parents, 'both English, and themselves born in the grotesquely elongated shadow, which they never rose sufficiently above history to leave, of that monstrous dwarf Queen Victoria.'

All this makes Fowles's novel, like Read's, a highly representative work. Mid-Sixties Eng. Lit. lay delicately poised, caught between a sometimes over-solid past and a highly uncertain future, between tradition and experiment, inertia and revolt, the whole ripe to be blown away by a type of book much less obviously concerned with form. Two of the most prophetic novels being written in 1966 were A.S. Byatt's *The Game* , eventually published in 1967, and Kingsley Amis's *I Want it Now* (1968). Each was a harbinger of what critics have come to know as the 'anti-Sixties novel', examining the spectacle of personal fulfilment and King's Road *chic* and finding only moral vacancy. *The Game*, for example, stars a pair of contending sisters, one of whom commits suicide when the other – a modish TV presenter-cum-novelist – cannibalises her life for the printed page. The possibilities advertised by the Sixties, swinging or otherwise, are, to Byatt, a horribly mixed blessing, simultaneously a means to advancement, a chance to shine and a fount of shallowness. Even in the quaint old world of literature, it turns out, the decade was ready to explode.

Times Literary Supplement, 2016

STRETCHING INTO TWILIGHT: LOOKING BACK ON THE SUMMER OF LOVE

JILL D'ALESSANDRO and COLLEEN TERRY, Eds. – *Summer of Love: Art, Fashion and Rock and Roll*

BILL DEMAIN, MIKE McINNERNEY and GILLIAN G. GAAR, Eds. – *Sgt Pepper at 50: The Mood, The Look, The Sound, The Legacy of The Beatles' Great Masterpiece*

Pink Floyd: Their Mortal Remains

One of the sharpest comments on the phenomenon known as the 'Summer of Love' can be found in the Frank Zappa and the Mothers of Invention long-player *We're Only In It For The Money*, issued in the spring of 1968. Something of Zappa's intentions may be glimpsed in its lavish front-cover pastiche of *Sgt Pepper's Lonely Hearts Club Band*, which on its release in June 1967 had topped the UK album chart for several months. Rather more can be inferred from the lyric sheet. If the tone of *Sgt Pepper* had been idealistic and forgiving, then Zappa's riposte is sarcastic and vindictive. Among a series of parodies of such West Coast Summer of Love house-bands as Arthur Lee's appropriately-named Love and the Jefferson Airplane, one might single out the track 'Flower Punk' in which the San Franscisco scene-sweller of the title is subjected to an antistrophic question-and-answer session:

> *'Hey punk, where you going with that flower in your hand?*
> *'I'm going down to 'Frisco to join a psychedelic band.'*

'Hey punk, where you going with that badge upon your shirt?'
'I'm going to the love-in to sit and play my bongos in the dirt.'

And so, incriminatingly on, to a tripped-out valedictory monologue in which Zappa's hippy, wondering what to do with the record royalties that will surely accrue from his descent on 'Frisco ('No, I'll buy a Corvette… No, I'll buy a Harley-Davidson' etc) eventually decides to put the money into real estate.

If to Zappa, the hippies – real and pretend – who flocked to San Francisco for the 'be-ins' and impromptu music festivals in which the early part of 1967 abounded were simply opportunists and bandwagon-jumpers, then to the Beatles' George Harrison, who might be thought to have helped create the whole movement in the first place, they were merely squalid and frightening. Stopping by in Haight-Ashbury, San Francisco, the epicentre of Sixties hippy-dom, in August 1967 Harrison, guitar in hand, is supposed to have wandered, troubadour-like, through the bead-laden and be-kaftaned throng singing the newly-composed Beatles song 'Baby You're a Rich Man.' According to the Beatles' publicist Derek Taylor, who was riding shotgun, Harrison's reaction was little short of disgust: the Haight, formerly the *locus classicus* of contemporary enlightenment, had become a magnet for 'ghastly drop-outs, bums and spotty youths.' When Harrison declined the offer of some STP – an extraordinarily potent psychotropic drug – the crowd turned nasty. Beatle and entourage made a hasty retreat. Clearly the Summer of Love's charms had already stolen away – if, that is, they had ever existed in the first place.

But what was the Summer Love, whose fiftieth birthday celebrations have already cranked into gear on both sides of the Atlantic? Where did it take place? What were its origins? Who devised it, and what were they hoping to achieve? The pat answer is that it was a counter-cultural youth (ish) movement taking in everything from music, fashion and aesthetics to sex, politics and psychology that sprang into existence on the West Coast of America and in certain exclusive quadrants of south-east England, burned brightly for a season or so only to be fatally disabled by its exposure to the cultural (and commercial) mainstream. As for chronology, you can take your pick from half-a-dozen high-points: the 'Gathering of the Tribes for a Human Be-in', convened in San Francisco as early as January 1967; the Monterey Festival (mid-June); the 14-hour Alexandra Palace freak-out (late April); Pink Floyd's 'Games for May' (12 May); the release of *Pepper* (1 June); a second Alexandra Palace 'love-in' (29 July) – all have some claims to constituting the moment when the 'Beautiful People' invoked by 'Baby You're A Rich Man' first advertised themselves to the world at large.

And already at least two of the conceptual problems that have dogged the Summer of Love from the moment the 'straight' media first noticed that it was taking place have begun to declare themselves. One is the level of confraternity – this could range from well-meaning collusion to straightforward collision – between Haight-Ashbury and a British end of the movement, which tended to oscillate between W11 and the King's Road. Another is the fatal influence of that 'straight' media on the Beautiful People's animating spirit and the devitalising effect of newspaper headlines and television exposes. 'They're selling hippy wigs in Woolworth's' drug-addled Danny famously laments towards the end of Bruce Robinson's *Withnail and I*. The film – co-produced by George Harrison, neatly enough – is set in the last months of 1969, but the point was being made in underground magazines at least two years before. At the heart of Zappa's demonology, after all, lurk the 'phony hippies', weekend tourists, keener on record-deals, buckskin jackets and obliging teenage girls than peace, love and freeing your inner self.

Though designed on the grand scale, and both accompanying exhibitions – the former at the San Francisco Museum of Fine Arts, the latter at the V&A – *Summer of Love* and *Pink Floyd: Mortal Remains* are very different books. The one is an exercise in psycho-geography, even extending to maps of central San Francisco and the locations of its 'head' shops; the other catalogues the history of a perennially successful English 'progressive rock' group, whose early records may be said to have shaped the Summer of Love's woozy, psychedelic and determinedly switched on sound. Taken together, their effect is highly syncretic, confirming the existence of two distinct countercultural movements that were separately at work on either side of the Atlantic while pursuing what were more or less the same ends and utilising what were, in some cases, very similar materials.

In each case, too, pre-history was vitally important. Dennis McNally's essay in *Summer of Love*, for example, sets out in well-nigh forensic detail the range of social, cultural and geographical factors that transformed the Haight in the early part of 1967: these take in everything from the foundation of the University of Berkeley's Free Speech Movement in 1964 and the opening of the Tape Music Centre the year before to the communal drug experiments of Ken Kesey's 'Acid Tests.' That certain parts of London weren't far behind is confirmed by Joe Boyd's contribution to *Mortal Remains*. Boyd, a significant figure in the mid-60s music scene and, among other distinctions, producer of Pink Floyd's first single 'Arnold Layne', detects foundation stones in the efforts to establish the 'London Free School' and the autumn 1966 musical 'happenings' in Powis Square, at which every fledgling 'underground' band in England from Hawkwind to the Pink Fairies seems to have appeared at one time or another. Shared influences tended to turn up in literature – the Beat Poets, Ginsburg especially, Tolkien (there was even a short-lived 'head' magazine called 'Gandalf's Garden'), Aldous Huxley's consciousness-raising – but they could also be found in the anti-nuclear protests of the previous decade and not giving a damn about Vietnam.

To the general public, on the other hand, bemused and intrigued by the preponderance of oddly-dressed people photographed pic-nicking in Hyde Park, the principal ornament of the Summer of Love was its music. If, half-a-century later, the 'psychedelic' (ie drug-propelled) pop of 1967 can seem broadly homogenous, a matter of chiming guitars, nursery rhyme lyrics and phasing effects, then this wasn't how it looked at the time, when the absolute superiority of home-grown product to American stylings was a critic's staple. As the late Ian Macdonald once pointed out (in an essay reprinted in *The People's Music* (2003) the early records of such West Coast luminaries as the Jefferson Airplane, Country Joe and the Fish and the Grateful Dead were essentially pieces of country blues played at deafening volume to disguise their innocuousness, 'the tinny shriek of treble-boosted Gibson guitars... the fret-squeaking rumble of overdriven Fender basses.' The real action lay east of the Atlantic, and *Sgt Pepper*, in particular, was received with almost reverential awe on the West Coast. The Airplane's Paul Kantner, hearing the first imported copy, declared that 'something enveloped the whole world at that time and it just exploded into a renaissance.'

While *Sgt Pepper at 50* does full justice to the labyrinthine recording process that brought the disc to completion – nearly four months of studio time was eventually needed for its 13 tracks – then it also hints at some of the difficulties that awaited popular music in the post-Pepper climate, where successful bands were no longer simply recorded but expensively and laboriously produced. If Pink Floyd were arguably one of the greatest casualties of this retreat to the studio – see, for example, their multi-million selling *The Dark Side of the Moon* (1973), in which spontaneity is cheerfully sacrificed for special effects – then in 1967 their loose, spaced-out improvisations were at the forefront of rock's avant-garde, and in some ways far closer to where it was 'at' than John, Paul, George and Ringo. There is even – given that both bands were at work in adjacent studios at EMI – the possibility of a degree of cross-fertilisation, and Macdonald's *Revolution in the Head: The Beatles' Records and the Sixties* (1994) note the existence of an unreleased 16-minute instrumental thought to have been inspired by the Floyd's *Piper at the Gates of Dawn*.

In another, excellent essay in *Mortal Remains*, Jon Savage addresses the self-evident conflict between the band's underground credentials and their management's desire for them to record hit singles. There was a real-life symbol of this *impasse* in the increasingly conflicted shape of Syd Barrett, their founding guitarist and principal song-writer, so scrambled by his intake of LSD that in late 1967 he was replaced by Dave Gilmour. Saluted by *Disc and Music Echo* as 'part and parcel of London's new underground' movement, their music was described by their co-manager as 'an environment.' There was talk of a desire to play in 'collective situations' rather than established venues, and a marquee that could travel the country called 'The Freak Out Comes to Town.' On the other hand, when the Freak Out left London it could run into trouble. Playing their left-field material in provincial clubs, where audiences expected to hear the hits of the day, Barrett & Co. frequently had pints of beer thrown at them.

All this suggests that the Summer of Love was not always exportable beyond its core base. Neither, as almost everybody involved in commemorating it concedes, could it survive the inevitable commercialising process that accompanied its discovery by the mainstream world. It wasn't only Derek Taylor who protested at the squalor of Haight-Ashbury in summer 1967. Boyd maintains that the London 'scene' lasted less a year, its demise epitomised by the imprisonment of the *International Times'* editor John 'Hoppy' Hopkins on drugs offences in early June. There are interesting parallels with the punk explosion of 1976, of which a friend of mine who played in the original Buzzcocks line-up remarked that 'it was over by the time the newspapers found out about it.' Certainly, much of the self-styled 'psychedelic music' now being re-packaged to mark the anniversary can look highly contrived, a matter of erstwhile mod, soul and rhythm and blues outfits hastily re-inventing themselves to suit the prevailing style with scant regard for authenticity.

Meanwhile, as the mass media goggled at the spectacle of 'Love-ins' and the BBC rushed to ban the Purple Gang's deeply inoffensive single 'Granny Take a Trip' (the trip in question being an annual jaunt to Hollywood to audition for the movies), the Summer of Love offered a beguiling prism for countless other forms of culture, both high and low. Bloomsbury historians have noted the sensationalising coverage that attended the publication of Michael Holroyd's two-volume biography of Lytton Strachey in 1967–68, in which Charleston and Ham Spray Cottage were reimagined as 'Abodes of Love' and the underlying assumption was, as Clive James once jokingly put it, that 'the Bloomsbury people were true *ur*-hippies.' The same point was being made of Tolkien's hobbits, puffing away at their pipe-weed in the Arcadian comfort of The Shire.

This, of course, was nonsense, and predictably the Bloomsbury diarist Frances Partridge, compelled to listen to what younger friends assured her was a high-point of modern popular art, filed some withering remarks about 'that feeble Beatles record' in which she saw 'little talent, or originality, no power to excite…' It seemed 'that this current philosophy of youth is above all passive' Mrs Partridge sniffed. As for *Sgt Pepper*, the apex of the Beatle's parabolic career, after which their prodigious collective genius could only dwindle and die, the twenty-first century listener who comes to it anew will probably note its profound air of wistfulness, often extending to outright melancholy, the cheery confidence of McCartney's 'Yes, I will admit it's getting better' straightaway cancelled out by Lennon's slyly counterpointed 'It can't get no worse.' Even here, in the bright morning of the Summer of Love, the long afternoon of the Sixties stretches inexorably away into twilight.

Times Literary Supplement, 2017

FIFTY YEARS OF *YELLOW SUBMARINE*

Like many a pop-cultural highlight from the Age of Aquarius, *Yellow Submarine* came about mostly by accident. Its public unveiling, at a gala premiere made tabloid-worthy by the fact that Paul McCartney arrived alone rather than accompanied by his long-term girlfriend Jane Asher, was also weighed down by paradox. Here, after all, was that guaranteed box office smash a 'Beatles film' in which the Fab Four only appeared in the closing frames – the previous 90 minutes were left to to cartoon representations of themselves – a celebration of Beatle-banter whose vocal parts were supplied by actors, and an undertaking in which the band took no interest at all until cinema audiences and won-over critics signified their approval. What had started out as an expedient ended up, rather to its own surprise, as a *bona fide* classic from the late Sixties psychedelic margin – John, Paul, George and Ringo demonstrating yet again that practically any base metal could be turned to gold once exposed to their potent, alchemical touch.

As for the expediency, *Yellow Submarine* began life late in 1967 as not much more than a contractual obligation. Rudderless, after the death of their manager Brian Epstein, and already up to their necks in the cash-haemorrhaging vanity project of the Apple Corporation, the Beatles were keenly aware that they owed United Artists – the sponsors of *A Hard Day's Night* (1964) and *Help* (1965) – a third film. As none of them by this stage could work up the faintest enthusiasm for another extended stint in front of the cameras, George Dunning's animation offered an ingenious route out of the deal. If there was a legal obligation to provide four new numbers for the accompanying L.P., then in the wake of the *Sergeant Pepper* sessions, the vaults were crammed with unreleased material, some of it of very doubtful quality. 'It'll do for the album' John Lennon is supposed to have quipped whenever some undercooked snippet was played back to him by the studio engineers: it was in this cynical, provisional or at least improvisatory spirit that the enterprise ground reluctantly into gear.

All this gave the soundtrack album – released early in 1969 – a determinedly makeweight air. Of the six full-length songs on its opening side, 'Yellow Submarine' had already featured on *Revolver* (1966) while 'All You Need is Love' was a standalone single from July 1967. Of the new material, Harrison's sarcastic 'Only a Northern Song' had been rejected from *Pepper*; 'All Together Now' was a throwaway McCartney knees-up recorded in a single session, and 'It's All Too Much' another minor Harrison piece left over from the Summer of Love. Only 'Hey Bulldog', a new Lennon number from February 1968, has anything like the charge and dynamism of the Beatles' best work, and in the absence of further sweepings from the studio carpet, side two was given over to George Martin's orchestral score. On the other hand, if the album could be safely characterised by the Beatles biographer Philip Norman as 'a dustbin for second-rate tracks', then the film itself is a startling late '60s confection, thoroughly imbued with the spirit of the age in which it was conceived, but always glancing back to the older world behind it: at once a state-of-the-art Sixties freak-out and an increasingly wistful survey of the foundations from which that phantasmagoria eventually crept.

Much of this naturally, was down to the spectacular range of talent assembled for the project. Dunning himself was a fortysomething veteran of the Beatles cartoon series sponsored by the ABC television company in the US. Screenwriter Erich Segal's later credits would include the sempiternal weepie *Love Story*. With Heinz Edelmann on board as art director, what had originally been conceived as a vehicle for Beatles songs – there are also full-length versions of 'Eleanor Rigby', ''Lucy in the Sky with

Diamonds', 'Nowhere Man' and 'When I'm 64' – swiftly transforms itself into something far more subtle and left-field, a complex juxtaposition of colour and sound, where the music harmonises with the animated landscapes on display, rather than, as it were, letting them play second fiddle.

Yellow Submarine opens in 'Pepperland', an idyllic, sub-oceanic utopia, whose elegant, music-fancying inhabitants are regularly entertained by their in-house orchestra, Sergeant Pepper's Lonely Hearts Club Band, and whose moral code – that standard Sixties embrace of tolerance, inclusiveness and affirmation – is set out in a series of word-statues ('Yes', 'Love', 'Now', 'OK' and so on.) Into this blissed-out Arcadia erupt the music-hating Blue Meanies, bossed by their wonderfully camp, kinky boot-adorned leader 'His Blueness' (voiced by the comedian Dick Emery) and his craven side-kick Max. Happily the escaping 'Young Fred', manages to reach Liverpool in the Yellow Submarine, alert the Beatles and, after various adventures in such underwater playgrounds as the Sea of Time, the Sea of Science, the Sea of Monsters and the Sea of Holes, bring them all-conqueringly back.

Bright, primary colours, wide-eyed Sixties sloganeering (the Blue Meanies' Sidewinder-style surface-to-air missile, known as the 'Glove' is, inevitably, disabled by having the 'G' removed), efflorescent foliage and endless green grass... One of the fascinations of *Yellow Submarine*, half-a-century on, is its strew of late-60s cultural references: George is regularly heard to remark that 'It's all in the mind' (a famous catch-phrase from the *Goon Show*); the Beatles' encounter with the 'nowhere man', Jeremy Hillary Boob PhD, in the Sea of Nowhere, has a puzzled Ringo observe that he 'must be one of these Angry Young Men' (at one point Jeremy refers to his forthcoming '*New Statesman* piece'); while the cigar placed in the mouth of a denizen from the Sea of Monsters is trailed by a bar or two of Bach's 'Air on a G String', in homage to the long-running Hamlet cigar ad. Visually, though, the effect is far more eclectic: kind of collage of the contending cultural styles that were around in the 1960s, many of them dating back to a period seventy or even eighty years before the piece was conceived.

Item one in this agglomeration is the Edwardian chic that distinguishes the Pepperland couture, its high collars, its embroidered waistcoats and flowing skirts, its cloth-capped children, its willowy women got up as Pallas Athena and its men looking as if they had just stepped off the Sovereign's Lawn at Cowes. Item two, alternatively, is the almost Wellsian hint of the late-Victorian scientific romance that hangs over the interiors of the submarine, with its gadgets and buttons, edging – once things begin to go wrong – into the world of the Heath Robinson contraption, all tangled wires, mysterious levers and cack-handed menace. Then there are the gestures in the direction of Eastern mysticism (usually inspired by George's presence) supported by sitar-driven excerpts from such Harrison numbers as 'Love You To' from *Revolver*. To this can be added imagery from the inter-war era (the dancing girls in the 'Lucy in the Sky With Diamonds' sequence are Twenties flappers with a marked resemblance to Isadora Duncan) a top-dressing of patented Sixties psychedelia – see, for example, the swirling montages that illustrate 'Only a Northern Song' – and bumper servings of the brand of Sixties surrealism that, while updating Lewis Carroll and Edward Lear, also betrays the influence of contemporary artists like Ronald Searle

While no single style predominates, then one of *Yellow Submarine*'s strongest debts is to the world of pre-1950s variety. If British popular music of the Sixties is saturated in the music hall tradition (see the Kinks or an album like the Small Faces' *Ogden's Nut-Gone Flake* from 1968), then the Beatles had ostentatiously staked out their claim to this territory with *Sergeant Pepper's Lonely Heart's Club Band*, of which McCartney remarked that 'I thought it would be nice to lose our identities, to submerge ourselves in the persona of a fake group. We could make up all the culture around it and collect all our heroes in one place.' *Pepper's* title-track is, as the Beatles scholar Ian McDonald points out, 'a shrewd fusion of Edwardian variety orchestra and contemporary 'heavy rock", the pier end entertainment of 1910 meeting the Jimi Hendrix Experience head-on. A year later, these influences are still going strong. 'Yellow Submarine' and 'All Together Now' are both communal, football terrace-inflected singalongs shading into the orbit of the novelty song, and there is a rather revealing moment towards the end of the film in which, John having dropped a high-brow reference to Einstein, Paul counters with a snatch of 'Any Old Iron', a piece of high-speed patter recorded by the variety hall titan Harry Champion (1865–1942) as long ago as 1911.

Not that McCartney would have come up with this line himself – like much of the heavily accented Scouse back-chat it was doubtless written by the (uncredited) Mersey poet Roger McGough. On the other hand, via his jazz band-leading father Jim, he would have known exactly who Champion was and appreciated why he fits so well into the film's cultural palette. Again, another of *Yellow Submarine*'s incidental tricks is its habit of referring back to Sergeant Pepper's iconographic cover. Marilyn Monroe's silhouette features in the proceedings, and one of 'Lucy's' dancing men, zealous guiding his partner across the floor, looks very like Max Miller. Here, as so often in the film, we can see Dunning's animators, though not working to the Beatles' direction, picking up conceits from bygone Beatles albums and developing them in ways of which – you assume – the band would have strongly approved. As for their public comments, Lennon's thoughts on the piece are characteristically double-edged, keen on Edelmann's art-direction while complaining about Segal's all-too accurately pastiched Beatle-talk and suggesting that at least some of the visual ideas were his own.

But the strongest twitch on the historical thread comes at the moment when the film fetches up on Merseyside. There follows an extraordinary piece of choreography in which 'Eleanor Rigby' plays above the ruins of a black-and-white cityscape, the only constant patch of colour provided by the wandering submarine. A Churchillian bulldog in a union jack coat squats before footage of a Remembrance Day parade. Factory chimneys, bare, rising streets, ancient cast-iron lampposts, tenement buildings and disused viaducts offer a backdrop to (mostly) solitary human figures – a man jabbering desperately in a telephone kiosk; a figure perched on the arched upper storey of a derelict building; a flock of city-suited businessmen in bowler hats perched beneath umbrellas on snow-covered rooftops. These, clearly, are the 'lonely people' of McCartney's vocal, perilously adrift in a representation of the world they came from: a Liverpool which even in the 1960s is struggling to break free from its Victorian past.

The sense of recent – and sometimes not so recent – history rises again in a scene in which the Beatles, after finessing their way back into Pepperland, hide out beneath the bandstand preparatory to donning their Sergeant Pepper gear and setting up the film's finale. Outside the slopes are patrolled by Tommy Gun-wielding Meanies while packs of guard-dogs yelp and search-lights roam back and forth: the atmosphere of a Second World War film, into which four amiable Liverpudlians in strange costumes seem mysteriously to have strayed.

Yellow Submarine ends with the real Beatles briefly clowning to camera, each bearing a souvenir of his journey to Pepperland: Paul has 'a little LOVE'; Ringo returns with half a hole; George brandishes the submarine's propeller; John, telescope held to his eye, announces that more Blue Meanies are in sight of the cinema. For all the willed raucousness, their days as a workable musical unit are coming to an end. Within 18 months – all four members of the band were last present in the same studio on 22 August 1969 for the sequencing of *Abbey Road* – the whole thing will be over. Half a century later, the animation in which they barely appear says far more about them and the world they inhabited than could ever have been predicted at the time. As a piece of pictorial art it brings off the difficult trick of looking both ways simultaneously: from one angle a snapshot of what the Sixties thought of the Sixties; from another a meditation on what the Sixties thought about the decades that had preceded it; a celebration of a thronged and tumultuous decade which doubles up as a melancholic farewell.

New Statesman, 2018

V. ENTHUSIASMS

ANNOTATING ORWELL

Why annotate Orwell's novels? One compelling answer is that we now have the freedom to do so. Orwell died in January 1950, meaning that all six of them came out of copyright in the UK at the start of this year. Transatlantic reprint programmes, based on the 95-years from first publication rule, will have to wait until as late as 2029. Here in Britain, on the other hand, a vault guarded by the seneschals of messrs Penguin Random House and its predecessor firms these past 70 years has just creaked open and any old aspiring editor or zealous foot-noter can go and wander about inside.

Another is that, in terms of the period detail which can weigh down the most evergreen classic, Orwell's fiction is beginning to show its age. This is especially true of the four pre-war novels, *Burmese Days* (1934), *A Clergyman's Daughter* (1935), *Keep the Aspidistra Flying* (1936) and *Coming Up For Air* (1939), each of which comes stuffed with references to Woodbines and de Reszkes (brands of cigarettes), the Boots Circulating Library, Express Dairies, gorblimey hats (a kind of Great War-era forage cap) and Dr Palmer (William Palmer, 1824–1856, the celebrated 'Rugeley Poisoner'.)

Meanwhile, even a reader thoroughly *au fait* with the minutiae of bygone urban life, its three-piece suites bought on the HP from Drage's furniture store or the 'joeys' (silver threepenny bits) at which the shop-girls sneer, may need a cipher to *Burmese Days*, whose off-duty colonial administrators, when not attending to the *memsahibs* and their *kit-kit* (tr. 'officious meddling'), sit gossiping about the Pegu Club, General Dyer, the Pagett MPs, dak bungalows and Smart & Mookerdum's bookshop in Rangoon. And all this is to ignore the frequent mention of magazines that no longer exist and long-superannuated library favourites such as Michael Arlen and William J. Locke.

Like the clerical protocols on which George Eliot dwells so lovingly in 'Mr Gilfil's Love Story' in *Scenes From Clerical Life*, much of this detail is merely incidental. It tells us about the world through which Orwell's characters move, rather than the mental processes which led him to create them: a series of landscapes which, in their paraphernalia, are not so very different from J.B. Priestley's or Patrick Hamilton's, to name only two novelists with whom his 1930 output is occasionally compared. In fact, Orwell's creative techniques are surprisingly tricksy, and one of the signature marks of a novel like *Coming Up For Air* is the game-playing that turns out to be going on beneath its surface.

Some of Orwell's playfulness takes in the simple act of character-naming. This is hardly ever arbitrary, much more likely, once the trails are pursued back into the compost of Orwell's early life, to involve symbolism, figurative sleight-of-hand, or sly references to friends and acquaintances. 'Winston Smith' is, naturally, a social hierarchy-transcending amalgam of Winston Churchill and everyman, 'Miss Mayfill', who declines to swell the collection plate in *A Clergyman's Daughter* belongs to the Victorian tradition of medics with names such as 'Slaughter' and 'Filgrave', but 'Bumstead, J, 2713', the prisoner rebuked by the telescreen in the Ministry of Love derives from a man named Jack Bumstead, whose brother George kept the grocery shop across the road from Orwell's parents' house at 36 High Street Southwold.

Similarly, several of the minor characters in *A Clergyman's Daughter* embody private jokes. 'Dr Gaythorne' comes from 'Gathorne-Hardy', the family name of the Earl of Cranbrook, a Suffolk magnate with whose sons Eddie and Robert Orwell had been at Eton. 'Old Mrs Pither', whose varicose-veined legs Dorothy Hare has squeamishly to anoint with embrocation, is Orwell's friend the poet Ruth Pitter with one altered consonant. This habit of cannibalising literary friends is a constant. As *Keep The Aspidistra Flying* was going through the press early in 1936, a storm blew up over the potential for libel. Victor Gollancz, Orwell's publishers, were particularly worried about the identification of 'Mr McKechnie', the fictional Gordon Comstock's boss, with the real-life Francis Westrope, Orwell's one-time employer at Booklovers' Corner in Hampstead. Writing to Gollancz's understrapper Norman Collins on 18 February while out on the journey that produced *The Road to Wigan Pier* (1937), Orwell insisted that:

> Mr McKechnie is not a real person... In the book 'Mr McKechnie' is described as an old man with white hair & beard who is a teetotaller & takes snuff. My late employer (Mr F.G. Westrope, 1 South End Rd, Hampstead, N.W.3) is a middle-aged man who is not a teetotaller & never takes snuff.

Orwell may have invented the Mr McKechnie who sits by the fire in his room above the bookshop drowsing over Thomas Middleton's *Travels in the Levant* – the journals of an East India explorer, first published in the early 1600s, the annotator gleefully notes – but he took his name from his fellow-writer Samuel McKechnie (1899–1979), author of *Popular Entertainment Through the Ages* (1931) and the Glasgow vernacular novel *Prisoners of Circumstance* (1934), to whose home in Stanmore Orwell was a regular visitor in his Hampstead days. The same is true of the retired public school master Porteous in *Coming Up For Air* who writes off Hitler as 'purely ephemeral' – not pillaged from a list of retired Eton beaks but, all the evidence suggests, from the poet Hugh Gordon Porteus (1906–1993), with whom Orwell was in contact during the time the novel was written.

The biographical tide that runs through each of Orwell's novels is not always readily apparent. With its surfeit of references to the Anglican controversialists of the 1930s, its knowledgeable glances at *Hymns Ancient and Modern* and correct clerical attire ('On Easter Sunday he was actually wearing a Gothic cope with a modern Italian lace alb' etc) *A Clergyman's Daughter* is a tribute to Orwell's religious side. This was the part of him that, while teaching at a private school in Hayes in 1932, could inform his Suffolk friend Brenda Salkeld that he had 'been painting a box with a picture of St Anselm (local saint) for the church bazaar' and that he had 'now communicated by the way – a real effort, on my part, for the service was at 6.45 a.m.'

It is also a highly reliable guide to the life Orwell was living – sequestered, resentful and by implication lovelorn – as he composed it. *A Clergyman's Daughter* was written during the first nine months of 1934, in an upstairs room at his parents' home on the Suffolk coast while recovering from a bad attack of pneumonia. Orwell had no great opinion of Southwold – the very thinly-disguised 'Knype Hill' of the novel – whose main thoroughfare is described as 'one of those sleepy, old-fashioned streets that look so ideally peaceful on a casual visit and so very different when you live in them and have an enemy or a creditor behind every door.' By and large, Southwold returned the compliment.

One clue to Orwell's relationship with the town lies, again, in the name of his heroine Dorothy Hare. 'Hare' comes from his paternal grandmother, but 'Dorothy' looks as if it belongs to a girl named Dorothy Rogers, the daughter of a garage proprietor in nearby Walberswick, Orwell's courtship of whom in the spring of 1934 eventually led to his being pursued over Southwold Common and assaulted by her outraged fiancé. Another lies in his treatment of an episode early on in the novel in which Dorothy Hare, out shopping in the High Street, finds herself caught up in the electioneering for a forthcoming parliamentary by-election.

The Knype Hill contest involves the triumph of the Conservative candidate Mr Blifil-Gordon, described as a director of the local sugar-beet factory, whose campaign song runs: 'Who'll save Britain from the Reds? Who'll put the beer back into your pot?' As it happens, there was a real by-election in northern Suffolk on 16 February 1934, resulting in the return of the Tory

National Government candidate Pierse Loftus for the Lowestoft division with a majority of 1,920 votes. Loftus (1877–1956) was, if not the kingpin of a sugar-beet factory, then something close to it: a director of Southwold's principal employer, the Adnams brewery and a prominent local personality.

The suspicion that Orwell was conducting what amounts to a vendetta against the Loftus family moves up a gear with the introduction, as part of his father's election cortege, of 'Walph' (ie 'Ralph') Blifil-Gordon, disparaged as 'an epicene youth of twenty given to the writing of sub-Eliot *verse libre* poems…' Two hundred pages later, Walph is said to have had two poems accepted by the arch-reactionary *London Mercury*. The original can only be Pierse's son Murrough, who five months after Loftus *père*'s arrival in the House of Commons, published a book of poems entitled *A Sword Unearthed*, of which the *TLS* reviewer remarked 'When Mr Loftus sings quite simply of his native Suffolk, his verse has charm and atmosphere… But it is only occasionally that he subdues his wilfulness to the genius of place.'

Meanwhile, there is the question of influence. Each of Orwell's novels has its presiding spirit – Maugham in *Burmese Days*, say, Wells in *Coming Up For Air* – but dig down below the topsoil of all six them and the writer you find there is George Gissing. Gissing (1857–1903), it is fair to say, is everywhere in Orwell. When Dorothy Hare spends a Christmas Day reading *The Odd Women* (1893) pressed up against a tree at Burnham Beeches, the inference is palpable: Dorothy, cast out of her father's house and reduced to teaching in a flyblown private school, is an odd woman herself. Like *New Grub Street* (1891), *Keep The Aspidistra Flying* is both a conspectus of the literary scene and a novel about the emotional consequences of poverty, or as Gordon bluntly puts it in one of his long, bitter harangues to his girlfriend Rosemary, 'You won't sleep with me, simply and solely because I've got no money.'

It is the same in *Coming Up For Air*, where the conversations between George Bowling's father Samuel and the latter's

Gladstone-fancying brother Ezekiel about late-Victorian politics echo Harvey Rolfe's sarcastic remarks about 'Empire' in *The Whirlpool* (1897), sparked off by a sit-down with Kipling's *Barrack Room Ballads*. As for *Animal Farm*, we know that Orwell was a fan of Gissing's early novel *Demos: A Story of English Socialism* (1886), whose hero is a working-class Londoner who inherits a large sum of money and uses it to establish an alternative community on egalitarian lines. The scheme withers and dies, prompting one of the workmen involved to lament that 'We're a poor lot and deserve to be worse treated than the animals that haven't the sense to use their strength.'

Above the choc-a-bloc terrain of influence and settled scores looms a wider architecture. Seventy years after his early death, what might be called the teleological approach to Orwell – starting with *Nineteen Eighty-Four* and tracking back in search of similarities – is becoming a critic's cliché. And yet each of the early novels carries an ominous prefiguration or two: the 'horrid little bomb of bell-metal' (ie the alarm clock) which awakens Dorothy Hare in the same way that the telescreen prods Winston into life, the ribbons of paper fluttering in the street outside the window of Gordon Comstock's bookshop that point the attentive reader towards the little eddies of wind 'whirling the dust and paper into spirals' in the street beyond Victory Mansions.

And then there is that fanatic absorption in death, or rather the spectral presence here, amid the ebb and flow of an ordinary enough English life in which Hitler and Stalin are still only bogey-figures in newspapers, the equivalent of ghostly knocking heard far away, of 'the dead.' 'My poems are dead' Gordon tells his solitary literary sponsor, Ravelston, in the course of a tremendous lecture about the futility of any kind of creative endeavour. 'I'm dead. You're dead. We're all dead people living in a dead world.' The same accusations clang through *Coming Up For Air*, to the point where Bowling, looking at Porteous as he reveals another layer of his exquisite detachment, thinks that '*He's dead*. He's a ghost. All people like that are ghosts.' Ten years later,

Winston picks up the baton. 'We are the dead' he informs Julia as they lie in bed in their love-nest above Mr Charrington's antique shop.

Like most of Orwell's fiction, *Nineteen Eighty-Four* has a buried sub-text, another kind of book trying desperately to get out from under the superstructure Orwell has wished on it. This is a paean to the 'golden country', the lost landscapes of rural Suffolk in which he had wandered with Brenda and Eleanor Jaques (and, you suspect, one or two other women) a decade and a half before the novel was written. As his friend Tosco Fyvel noted, Orwell tended to let himself go stylistically whenever he tried to link his love of nature with his feelings for women, and the passages describing Winston and Julia's rendezvous in the countryside are strongly reminiscent of one or two of his letters to Eleanor from the early 1930s remembering assignations in the Suffolk verdure.

Animal Farm turns out to be another novel within a novel, in which, at a slight remove from the overthrow of Farmer Jones and the betrayal of the regime set up in his place, something else is stirring. One question worth asking of this devious and meticulously plotted fable is: when exactly is it set? Though published in 1945 and satirising the principal highlights of Soviet history between 1917 and 1943 (its final scenes can be related to the Tehran Conference) the novel's historical framework returns it to a much earlier time. Manor Farm is entirely unmechanised and there is no mention of motorised transport, while Mr and Mrs Jones's domestic interiors are a matter of 'looking glasses, the horsehair sofa, the Brussels carpet, the lithograph of Queen Victoria.'

Elsewhere there is talk of 'gentleman farmers', a social category that went into sharp decline after the Great War, 'low-crowned bowler hats', governess carts and a riot of incidental detail that seems to date the fictional proceedings (as opposed to their political equivalent) to the pre-1918 era. The periodicals that the pigs take in – *John Bull* and *Titbits* – once their credentials to farm ownership are established are staples of the Edwardian magazine rack. Even 'Mr Whymper', their double-crossing legal man, takes his name from a celebrated Victorian mountaineer.

The suspicion is that while anxious to attack what he regarded as a corrupt ideology designed to thwart the desires of ordinary people, Orwell has quietly established the novel in the world of his own childhood, much of which was spent in South Oxfordshire before and during the Great War. 'Willingdon', for example, the nearest town to Manor Farm, can be identified with Henley-on-Thames. As well as using a gang of insurrectionary animals to bring down the Soviet Communism, Orwell is also in hot pursuit of what may, in the end, be a yet more elusive quarry: the small but irresistible matter of his bygone self.

Times Literary Supplement, 2021

READING THE JAM

Forty years ago this month the members of the Jam – three late adolescents from Woking, Surrey, named Paul Weller (guitar and vocals) Bruce Foxton (bass and vocals) and Rick Buckler (drums) – could be found in Oxford Street's Stratford Place studios laying down tracks for their debut album, *In The City*. The recording process was quick-fire and experimental – some of the backing vocals were apparently recorded in a lift between floors – and in keeping with the rough and ready working practices of the 'new wave' of popular music then hitting the nation's record racks, the whole project was wrapped up in a bare eleven days. Come early May the band appeared on *Top of the Pops* to promote their first single before embarking on a 36-date national tour.

In their late '70s and early '80s heyday, the Jam were arguably the most successful indigenous pop act in Britain. Of their 17 hit singles, three went straight into the charts at Number One; four of their six studio albums made the top ten. Despite a smattering of female fans, they were mostly a boys' band and, more than that, a working-class boys' band: the atmosphere at their teeming and chaotic live concerts was essentially that of a football terrace. David Cameron, who professed himself an admirer of 'The Eton Rifles' (1979), a song about a Right to Work march that passed by the gates of Eton College to be barracked by the young gentlemen within, was sharply rebuked by Weller with the comment 'What part of it didn't he get?'

Four decades later, it is difficult to convey the sheer visceral excitement of those early appearances. I can remember seeing them on *Marc*, the late-afternoon television programme fronted by Marc Bolan, a superannuated glam-rock star who was shortly to die in a car-crash. Bolan, clad in a leopard-skin jump-suit, is clearly taken aback by his guests, so much so that he has to consult a button-badge to remind himself who they are. Leaping around the stage like outsize frogs bounding from one lily pad to the next, the boys, dressed in sub-fusc suits and black-and-white co-respondent's shoes, perform their second single 'All Around the World', a tumult of chiming chords, screeching feed-back and bawled lyrics about 'youth explosions', at such a pace that, by the closing seconds, Buckler's drum kit has begun to disintegrate.

The Jam's sound was initially characterised as a kind of Mod revivalism, much influenced by mid-Sixties acts such as the Who, while sharpened by the newfound punk aggressiveness brought to British pop by the Sex Pistols, the Clash and Buzzcocks. Throughout their career, they contrived to remain manifestly up-to-date while always harking back to the bygone classics of Lennon and McCartney and the Kinks' Ray Davies. The songs – the vast majority of them written by Weller – are, in no particular order, about love, violence, youth, social observation, class, identity and politics, the latter tendency reaching a high-point in the Thatcher-baiting 'Going Underground' (1980) and 'Town Called Malice' (1982) . They are also oddly poetic, infused with what, for the time and the place, was a highly distinctive brand of romanticism, and above all determined to put their words to work in the service of the music.

Interviewed in *About the Young Idea*, the DVD that accompanied 2015's commemorative exhibition at Somerset House, the always diffident Weller suggests that his 'literariness' only began to declare itself on *All Mod Cons*, the 1978 album usually thought by critics to mark their transformation from New Wave also-rans to major-league contenders. In fact the lyrics of 1977's *This Is The Modern World* are rife with literary allusion. The limpid, dreamy 'Tonight at Noon', for example, borrows from Adrian Henri (thanked in the sleeve-notes) while 'Standards', a routine lament about the system grinding you down ends with the fiery couplet 'And ignorance is strength, we have God on our side/Look you know what happened to Winston.' 'Winston', it soon becomes clear, is *Nineteen Eighty-Four*'s Winston Smith.

Weller's Orwell fixation is one of his most attractive characteristics. It can be seen in the Beatle-influenced single 'Start' (its octave-jumping bass line robbed from 'Taxman'), where the assurance that it's not important 'It doesn't matter if we never meet again/What we have said will always remain' and that 'if we can communicate for two minutes only it will be a *start*' shows the influence of *Homage to Catalonia*, and it can be teased out of 'Tales From the Riverbank', a B-side from 1981, with its references to 'this golden country', where the protagonist 'woke at sunrise, went home at sunset.' This returns us to the scene in *Nineteen Eighty-Four* where Winston, rendezvousing with Julia for some *plein air* frolics in a patch of woodland somewhere to the west of London, tells her that 'It's the golden country – almost... A landscape I've seen sometimes in a dream.'

Nearly every Jam album, if closely enough inspected, yields up its cache of book-world reference. *All Mod Cons*' 'Billy Hunt', about a teenage fantasist who yearns to grow bionic arms, after which 'the whole world's gonna wish it weren't born' is first cousin to Keith Waterhouse's *Billy Liar* (1957); 'Fly', a wistful love song from the same album, nods to *Peter Pan*; 'Absolute Beginners', a single from 1981, robs its title from Colin MacInnes's novel. At the same time, Weller's literariness is much more than a matter of name-checking his private library. Rather, it consists of a writing style that mingles down to earth reportage and idiom ('Saturday's Kids live in council houses/Wear V-neck shirts and baggy trousers') with what sometimes amounts to an almost baroque self-consciousness (sex to the middle-aged drudge in 'Private Hell' is recalled as 'the occasions he lies upon you') to create something that can, in the end, be deviously ornate.

'Billy Hunt', for instance, has a sinewy, alliterative line about Billy needing to 'satisfy any whim that I wanted to'. The subject of 'Down in the Tube Station at Midnight', about to be kicked to pieces by a gang of fascist thugs ('They smelled of pubs and Wormwood Scrubs, and too many right-wing meetings') approaches a slot-machine ('I fumble for change, and pull out the Queen, smiling, beguiling') to mint an image that not only connects with him with the face on the coin but gestures back at the character in the Beatles' 'Penny Lane' in whose 'pocket is a portrait of the Queen.' 'Beat Surrender', the final single from November 1982, and intended, Weller recalled, 'as a letter to my audience', invited the fans to 'succumb' to the music's adrenalin rush before finally assuring them, in language taken straight out of a Victorian *billet doux*, that 'I am yours and will always be beholden to/The Beat Surrender.'

And then there is the romanticism – dense, doomy and sometimes literally fugitive, in which the other half is urged 'Let's disappear love, let's fly away/Into the demi-monde, into the twilight zone' ('Fly'), recommended to try 'the tranquillity of solitude' ('That's Entertainment') and where being young – a natural theme for a singer who first entered a recording studio at the age of 18 – consists of stealing 'the silent wind that made us feel free... the greenbelt fields that made us believe' ('Thick as Thieves.') If much of the Jam's output was aimed at conciliating the communality of its audience, then a fair proportion was bent on exposing it, and some of Weller's best songs are about being on your own, searching out 'the place I love' which is a 'million miles away from here' ('The Place I Love'), maintaining your autonomy in that classic Mod melting-pot 'the crowd.'

Many of these themes come together in 'Tales From the Riverbank', which takes both title and setting from Kenneth Graham but is also informed by the brand of Sixties pop-pastoralism begun by the Syd Barrett-era Pink Floyd with *Piper at the Gates of Dawn* (1967). Here, above a meandering bass line, with occasional brass flourishes and drum rat-tats, Weller announces that he intends to 'Bring you a tale from the pastel fields/Where we ran where we were young/This is a tale from the water meadows/Spreading love and joy into your heart... A place of hope in an endless time.' Curiously, the version printed in *Suburban 100: Selected Lyrics* (2007) omits what might be regarded as the most crucial moment – a faintly doleful Weller deducing that 'now you don't get so many to the pound.'

By late 1982 Weller had had enough – enough of the adulation, enough of the fan-frenzy and more than enough of being considered a spokesman for a youth movement he didn't remember starting in the first place. Breaking up the band – to the considerable distress of Foxton and Buckler – he went off with his friend Mick Talbot to form the Style Council, whose jazzy and later classically-tinged records most Jam fans heartily disliked, before beginning an immensely successful solo career. Together with such contemporaries as The Fall's Mark E. Smith and Steven Morrissey, he remains a classic example of what might be called pop's buried literary sensibility – the teenager with no formal education to speak of (Weller, who left school at 15, rated himself 'really thick') who has somehow managed to find out about books and use them to irradiate his view of the world. Few British songwriters from that late-70 and early '80s golden age brought such articulacy to the three-minute pop song, so fervently proclaimed the power of words or stayed so close to an audience whose ideals they genuinely wished to share.

Times Literary Supplement, 2017

THE PASSING OF PRESCOTT

The 'Cross-bencher' column of the old-style *Sunday Express* had a patented formula for checking out the ambitions of any politician who strayed onto its radar. What thoughts, it would innocuously enquire, were crowding into the head of Mr X, the member for Lymeswold Central, as he stepped briskly into the committee room this bleak December forenoon? To adapt this for the modern age, what thoughts are crowding into the head of the Right Honourable – prospectively Lord – Prescott, retiring member of parliament for Hull East, this bright May morning as he prepares not only to cast his vote but to relinquish a role in British political life that was first taken up all of forty years ago?

One fact that Mr Prescott will very probably reflect upon is the profound change that has come upon the House of Commons since he first started making his presence felt in it back in 1970, as part of a leftist-leaning Labour intake that included Lord (as he now is) Kinnock and Dennis Skinner. There were genuine Tory 'knights of the shire' – Sir Harry Legge-Bourke and Rear-Admiral Sir Charles Morgan-Giles– still deedily at large in the Commons tea-rooms in those days. The Labour back-benches groaned under the weight of superannuated trades unionists, and no South Yorkshire nomination changed hands with the National Union of Mineworkers' nod. Tribalism was triumphant, modernising influences suspect, and the gnarled back-bencher once asked if he would be voting for Roy Jenkins in a leadership election is supposed to have replied 'Nay lad, we're all Labour here.'

Four decades later, and whatever the ramifications of tonight's result, the Commons is set for one of the greatest personnel changes in its history, in which as many as 40 per cent of its seats will have new occupants. Onto its back-benches will sweep a tide of Tory management consultants and millionaires, Labour barristers and local government officials and Lib Dem university lecturers and technocrats – young (for the most part), presentable, tractable, trained up by the party managers in the art of answering tricky questions in a relaxed yet forceful manner. None of them it can safely be predicted, will be anything like John Prescott.

Zealously unpicked and reconstituted by the nation's journalists these past thirteen years and more, endlessly crawled over by ideologues of right and left, disparaged by feminists, acclaimed (sometimes) by the mysterious entity known as 'the ordinary working man', Prescott's progress has all the elements of a modern myth, in which each episode is capable of proving some salutary moral about the age we inhabit, and each supplementary character eventually declares him- or herself as a figure of altogether gargantuan import. There is old Bert Prescott, the railway signalman who began it all, first estranged from his thrusting young son but eventually reconciled.

There are the teachers of Brinsworth Manor School and their failure to secure him the grammar school scholarship he craved. There is the stewarding job for Cunard, ferrying gin-and-tonics to Anthony Eden's cabin ('a real gentleman' according to Prescott). Less picturesquely, but testimony to Mr Prescott's burning ambition to make his mark, there is the trip to Ruskin College, Oxford and the Hull University economics degree. H.G. Wells might not have liked the reality of Mr Prescott, but he would known where he came from and relished the spectacle of his ascent.

And, taken in the round, Mr Prescott has always borne an uncanny resemblance to a Wells hero: come from nowhere; barrelling on to no-one quite knows where; moody, prejudiced and impetuous, but also bonhomous, modest and mundane, liked and despised in equal shares, as loyal to his party as to himself. Like the family described in Hilary Mantel's memoir *Giving Up The Ghost*, he had aspiration but no aspirates. No one could deny the upwardly-mobile class warriors of the post-war era their materialism, modern historians tend to suggest, given the crucible of debt and deprivation in which it had been forged. There was a poignant symbolism, consequently, in this tribune of the people deploying two Jaguars (one of them admittedly government-issue) in a movement where one would sometimes have been considered too many. With Prescott, Socialism was not only moving down the road – that famous 250 yard dash to a conference hall where he was booked to discuss public transport policy – but also, indisputably, with the times.

But then symbolism has woven itself through every aspect of Mr Prescott's career, like bindweed through a lawn. The most obvious mark of his larger-than-life quality is the extraordinary number of nick-names he attracted. Most senior politicians make do with one, or at most two. James Callaghan's were 'Sunny Jim', because of his supposedly equable temperament, and 'Farmer Jim', on account of the rolling Sussex acres where he spent his weekends. Prescott, on the other hand, accumulated at least six: 'Prezza', to begin with; 'Two Jags' (a reference to the car-fleet); 'Jabba The Hut' (*The Return of the Jedi*'s outsize villain); 'Two Jabs' (after attacking a protesting farmer who had thrown an egg at him); 'Two Shags' (a discreditable incident in his private life'); and even 'No Jobs', coined by this newspaper after his lost his department in a cabinet reshuffle of 2006 but contrived to retain both the residence and the perquisites associated with the title. There are probably others.

Only an ingrate would suggest that the soubriquets came in inverse proportion to the political achievement. Certainly, the outsize portfolio he was handed in 1997, as head of the newly created Department for Environment, Transport and the Regions, produced surprisingly little return. There was talk – but only talk – of something called an 'integrated transport strategy'. A scheme for regional assembles had to be abandoned. But he was an indefatigable critic of the rail companies and an assiduous Kyoto lobbyist, and later worked with the Milliband brothers on the govermment's post-Kyoto agenda. And then there is the unarguable fact that throughout this period the responsibilities with which he was invested were much less important than what he was supposed to represent. What he was supposed to represent was New Labour's link with 'Labourism', those (metaphorically) cloth-capped traditionalists appalled by the modernising line being taken by the party's new leaders, after John Smith's death in 1994, but prepared to lend support (and funding) if power could be delivered. Even greater than this, perhaps, was the responsibility of keeping Gordon happy with Tony and *vice versa*.

Power was duly delivered, but the price was considerable, not least to Prescott himself. To browse the political memoirs of the 1990s and early 2000s is to appreciate quite how much he was disdained by the people he came up against. Even quite nice politicians detested him. 'A terrible man, absolutely awful and a hypocrite' John Major pronounced, shortly before the 1997 General Election. Coming across him at a *Spectator* party at around this time, Woodrow Wyatt's daughter Petronella found him practically lachrymose. 'He got very drunk. He said he hated Blair and the people around him. "They insist on coaching me to talk grammatically and 'posh' and I don't want to speak grammatically." Wyatt assured him that "You do it like Ernie Bevin. It's all pretty coherent."'

This, alas, is to ignore the tortured syntax of *Private Eye*'s 'Let's parler Prescott' column, and the story – no doubt apocryphal, but these things stick – of applicants for jobs on *Hansard* being required to listen to one of the Deputy Prime Minister's speeches and see if they could understand what he was saying. It gave rise, at any rate in Labour Party circles, to what journalists christened 'the Prescott Defence'. Last used by supporters of the former speaker, Michael Martin, after his enforced departure from office, it consists of declaring that any criticism of politicians with working-class origins on grounds of articulacy was simply an expression of class prejudice. Mr Prescott's detractors, alternatively, declared that class prejudice had nothing to do with it, and that ministers of the crown, from whatever social class, who presumed to address millions of people on television should be able to do so coherently.

Such disputes gesture at Mr Prescott's one unique talent: his ability to create newspaper headlines, to reduce the small matter of government policy and its presentation to the much larger matter of himself. It is an axiom that controversial politicians attract controversy, but Mr Prescott's serial exposure at the hands of the press over the past 13 years is unparalleled in modern political history. Were he to attend the Brit awards, it could be guaranteed that a radical musician would throw water over him. Campaign-trail eggs descended on his shoulders with a kind of homing instinct, and if fists had to be thrown, then he was the man to throw them. The public money used to pay the council tax on his government flat; Ms Tracey Temple, his diary secretary, adulterously entertained at his official residence; the sexual harassment claims; the two toilet seats in as many years that featured in his expenses claim… in the end the inexorability of the Prescott disclosures suggested that they derived not from bad luck, or even malicious enquiry, but from some deep-rooted psychological flaw, like those masochistic English professors whose relish at having the mistakes in their work pointed out is so acute that you wondered why they allowed them there in the first place,

All this has a figurative significance well beyond the traditional exploits of larger than life politicians: these are usually back-bench mavericks rather than king-makers and vote-corallers who spend a decade and a half at the very highest levels of political life. More so than any politician of the modern era, Mr Prescott was a man caught between a rock and a hard place. The rock was New Labour and the hard place was the political tradition that bred him. Both, curiously enough, look unlikely to survive the events of the next 24 hours. Meanwhile, there is Prescott himself, whose exploits over the past twenty years might be thought to demand a kind of commemorative frieze or tapestry, its key scenes picked out by a squad of twenty-first century needlewomen in countless strands of blue and red.

The punch-ups! The shags! The speeding fines! The packed bags and the furious wife on the doorstep (the long-suffering Mrs Prescott's part in the saga almost demands a frieze of its own)! In the end, one feels a queer kind of sympathy over the paradoxes of Mr Prescott's career. He was New Labour's conscience, and its serial embarrassment, its pacifier and its pugilist, its throwback and the guarantor of its future, the guardian of its citadel and the keeper of its folly. As he casts his vote this morning in Hull East, Mr Prescott may feel that these roles were too many for any single politician to sustain, let alone the railwayman's son from Prestatyn whom the wicked modernisers wanted to talk posh.

Independent, 2010

AT THE ORWELL STATUE

Here at the top of Regent Street, amid concertina traffic and lowering skies, the rain is coming down hard. Together with the Orwell Foundation's director Professor Jean Seaton, I make a beeline for the porch of All Souls, Langham Place, but find it occupied. As in an Anthony Powell novel, to which, as Jean quickly notes, this early November afternoon bears a particularly strong resemblance, unfamiliar figures begin to reconstitute themselves into recognizable shapes. Like Widmerpool hastening through the Berkshire mist, the people huddled beneath the porch reveal themselves to be Orwell's adopted son, Richard Blair, the BBC's media correspondent Amol Rajan and a camera crew. After a bit Richard joins us in the rain. "I tried to tell them about the girls' school and the lunatic asylum", he explains, recalling his father's bracing put-down about employment in the BBC, "but they didn't seem terribly interested." We press on over the grainy piazza through the plate-glass portal of New Broadcasting House.

Aubrey Beardsley once filed a drawing of some sinister, black-clad opera-goers to the *Yellow Book*, entitled 'The Wagnerites'. What do the Orwellians, here assembled to witness the unveiling of Martin Jennings's statue of the great man, look like *en masse*? As might be expected, BBC trusties (Director General Tony Hall, Alan Yentob, Melvyn Bragg, Andrew Marr) predominate, but there is space for old-Labour front-benchers (Lord Kinnock's ID remains unclaimed on the table, alas), scholars and biographers, keen-eyed delegates from the Orwell Society and Richard Blair's children and grandchildren. A venerable figure surveying the throng from a chair in the Media Café turns out to be Peter Davison, now ninety-one, doyen of Orwell Studies and the editor of the twenty-volume *Complete Works* (plus addenda). We discuss just how many people still inhabit the planet who can be said to remember Orwell, nearly sixty-eight years after his death, but cannot get the figure beyond ten.

The total includes an elderly nephew and two nieces, the centenarian Anne Olivier Bell, whose memories of Orwell proposing marriage to her in 1946 – followed by a letter in which he canvassed the advantages of being the widow of a literary man – could be heard in the recent Radio 4 documentary *George Orwell: Back at the BBC*, the ninety-five-year-old Janetta Parlade, last surviving attendee of his wedding to Sonia Brownell in 1949, and Janetta's daughter, the artist Nicky Loutit, who recalls being taken by her mother to what was effectively Orwell's deathbed at University College Hospital. At seventy-three, Richard – now being hauled away to face yet another bank of cameras – is the youngest of this select band. From a vast rectangular screen, so dramatically enlarged as to achieve a Big Brother-like dominance of the room and everything in it, the famous BBC photograph of Orwell at the microphone stares down.

Irony, meanwhile, is stalking the premises with all the determination of the flesh-pressing Director General, Lord Hall. First there is the fact that Orwell's two-and-a-bit years working for the Eastern Service, initially at No 55 Portland Place later at a satellite address at 200 Oxford Street, produced no lasting record of his voice. Then there is his string of wounding remarks about administrative chaos, vanishing audiences and the waste of time and public money (an exception was BBC cuisine, which Orwell pronounced *marvellous*.) Seen in the round, as Desmond Avery points out in his excellent little book *Orwell at the BBC in 1942* (Garth Press), these criticisms can be over-cooked. One might note a broadcast from March 1942, outlining the schedule of a series called 'Through Eastern Eyes', in which Orwell assures his listeners how happy it makes him to be helping organize 'broadcasts which I believe can be really helpful and constructive at a time like this – to the country in which I was born and with which I have many personal and family ties'.

Further evidence to gladden the hearts of the Corporation's publicists can be found in the pleasure he took in assembling groups of talking-heads who ornamented such Eastern Service innovations as 'New Words' (this covered the highly Orwellian topic of neologisms thrown up by the Second World War), 'Great Dramatists' (including T.S. Eliot on Dryden) and *Voice*, a literary magazine of the ether, whose surviving scripts may be thought to challenge another oft-quoted obiter dicta from his BBC days, that 'poetry on the air sounds like the muse in striped trousers'. In the other famous photograph from his war-time broadcasting days, in which he hovers at the back of a semi-ellipse of distinguished contributors that includes the Sinhalese poet Tambimuttu, Una Marson, Mulk Raj Anand and William Empson, pocket handkerchief spilling from the pocket of his subfusc suit, he looks positively jaunty.

Back at New Broadcasting House, where the abundant BBC sandwiches show no signs of running out – a surplus that even Tony Hall finds remarkable – it is time to quit the Media Café for the unveiling. The site chosen for this eight-foot-high bronze leviathan, still concealed behind billowing black curtains, is a windy corridor to the left of the revolving doors: destination of choice, we are reliably informed, for the Corporation's smokers. The small crowd assembled behind the crash-barriers is easily outnumbered by the guests. As the breeze whips through the culvert and the picture-snapping mobile phones rise and fall, Baroness Whitaker pays tribute to her late husband Ben, whose idea this was, and Richard Blair, all thought of girls' schools and lunatic asylums forgotten, offers tactful remarks about his father's resignation letter of November 1943. Not only was Orwell keen to start work on the book that became *Animal Farm*, Richard volunteers, but looming in the background was the small matter of his own adoption.

As for the statue – briskly uncovered on a count of three – most of those present seem to agree it isn't bad. Among other physical characteristics, Jennings has got the six-foot-four

Orwell's stoop, his narrow-chested spindliness and the parted pompadour wave of his notoriously cheap haircuts. A preliminary scheme to portray him in jacket and shirt sleeves was vetoed by Richard on the grounds that his father always appeared in suit, collar and tie. Similar refinements were made to the cigarette that dangles from the fingers of his right hand after those in the know lobbied for a hand-rolled dog-end. There are Chaplinesque hints of the variety hall comedian and the shop-walker, but also echoes of the Gallic forebears on his mother's side that Anthony Powell invoked when he wrote that Orwell resembled 'one of those fierce melancholy French workmen in blue smocks pondering the meaning of life at the zinc counters of a thousand *estaminets*'.

Lord Hall, a broken reed in technology's grasp, announces that this is, additionally, a talking statue and that a phone with the correct app installed will, when held up to it, transmit what purports to be Orwell's own view of his presence here, voiced by Daniel Day-Lewis. There are to be more speeches back in the café. A promising discussion with Andrew Marr about the BBC's effect on Orwell's later work is cut short by a fan jumping the crash barrier and asking – asking Marr, that is – for a selfie. If continued, it would probably have taken in the real Room 101 that existed at 200 Oxford Street, the rabbit-hutch offices in which Winston Smith and colleagues sit airbrushing non-persons out of history, the dense, bureaucratic fog that hangs over *Nineteen Eighty-Four* like a shroud and one or two of the fleeting humanistic moments in which some kind of warmth rises from a landscape generally plunged below zero. Informed judges, for example, usually insist that the proletarian woman heard singing beyond the window of Winston and Julia's love nest grew out of Orwell's memory of gangs of BBC charwomen in full voice as, mops and buckets in hand, they moved off along the Corporation's grimy corridors.

Back inside the crowd is thinning out, although great heaps of sandwiches remain. Following Jean Seaton, in her capacity as the BBC's official historian, Marr turns in a rip-roaring speech, bites every hand held out to feed him, reproduces every injurious remark he can find in the Collected Works, assures us that Orwell would have deplored this public memorial and certainly have voted for Brexit, asks for solidarity with the BBC's much-oppressed Persian Service and draws our attention to the quote engraved on the wall next to the statue: 'If liberty means anything, it is the freedom to tell people what they do not want to hear'. A suspicion that has been sneaking up on me ever since I set foot in the building is finally confirmed. What we have here, I tell myself as Messrs Hall and Yentob glide away, is a case of the BBC stealthily propagandizing on its own behalf – and none the worse for that. Outside, it is still raining. The great and the good gather up their umbrellas and depart and the piles of sandwiches moulder in their trays.

Times Literary Supplement, 2017

WHY REVIEW BOOKS?

One Friday afternoon 24 years ago next month – you can see how long these things rankle – I was sitting at my desk in the marketing department of messrs Ernst & Young, chartered accountants, when the phone rang. The caller was the man who commissioned the fiction reviews for the *Sunday Times*. 'I'm very sorry' he began, 'but there's a really bad review of your novel in Sunday's paper.' How bad was really bad, I wondered, trying to find some crumb of comfort in this weekend-wrecking news. '*Really* bad' my friend explained. 'I mean, he absolutely hates it.' There was nothing left to do, except to exchange a few broken civilities, fret through the next 36 hours and nervously reconnoitre the *Sunday Times* books section until such time as my eye alighted on a paragraph assuring its readers that the darling work on which I had lavished so much care and Roget-roughaged attention was 'about as much use as a one-legged man in a butt-kicking competition.' If there was any comfort, it lay in the thought of a wound soon healing into a proud, professional scar. I, too, am a book-reviewer, I told myself, and if you live by the sword, you must expect to die by it as well. Not for nothing are the critics in novels about early-Victorian literary life given names like Bludyer and Slasher.

The first book I ever reviewed (a rather good avant-garde novel by Sue Roe called *Estella: Her Expectations*) was for *The Spectator*, a small matter of 37 years ago. The last (John le Carré's new one) was for *Private Eye*, just the other week. Filling up the space between these two marker-flags are a whole lot more, for the *London Magazine*, *Encounter* and the *London Evening Standard*, and later on the *Independent*, the *Guardian* and the *Sunday Times*, before a swerve into more exotic ports of call like *Political*

Quarterly, the *Wall Street Journal*, *New Republic* and the UAE-based *National*, while never forgetting such reliable coigns of book-world vantage as the *Times*, *The Spectator* the *New Statesman* and the *Literary Review* – a couple of thousand, maybe, running, in the peak years (1988–1993, say), at the rate of three or sometimes four a week. If this sounds like hack-work on an heroic scale, then it should be said that many a bygone literary career more exalted than mine throws up similar statistics: Graham Greene's biographers calculate that he reviewed nearly a thousand books in the 1930s alone, and if the sketch of the moth-eaten, bedsit-bound drudge in Orwell's 'Confessions of a Book-Reviewer' isn't precisely a self-portrait it is close enough to the kind of life that Orwell was leading in his apprentice years to stop any Grub Street romanticiser dead in his tracks.

Naturally, there are distinctions to be drawn, for these were not all the same kind of review, written at the same kind of length or for the same kind of audience. As any long-time adornment of what the Victorian novelist George Gissing used to call 'the valley of the shadow of books' knows, and sometimes to their cost, you approach the task in one way for the *Daily Express* and in another way for *Transactions of the Arthur Machen Society*. In reviewing for the *London Review of Books* you may scarcely mention the book at all. In reviewing for a daily newspaper, any injurious gossip that the author may throw up will be warmly welcomed. Four hundred words may be too much for *The Tablet* and 4,000 too little for the *Times Literary Supplement (TLS)*. At the same time, the esteem in which you are held varies wildly from outlet to outlet. At the *TLS* a tribe of highly intelligent editors will queue up to offer tactful suggestions and discreet amendments and undertake to send you a proof in the week before publication. At the other end of the scale, the woman who used to edit the books page at the *London Evening Standard* 30 year ago, would, when pressed for space, simply lop off the last two paragraphs. And at all times, at any rate at the popular end of the market, comes the constant reminder that what you do is not really serious, there on sufferance, always ripe for displacement if some bigger fish – Brexit, an interview with Margaret Atwood – comes surging into the pool.

If this is the landscape in which book reviewing takes place, then how has it changed in the 37 years since I first took up residence there? And what are the first principles that might be supposed to animate it? Grimly surveying the phantom library acquired since the days of the first Thatcher administration, I suspect that, over the years, the impulse that led me to pick up the pen separates out into five distinct categories. The trip to A.N. Wilson's office at *The Spectator* was undertaken out of straightforward intoxication, the idea that here was a hugely glamorous professional stage on which, if you had the gumption and the talent, you might be able to play a part. Later came the necessity of making a splash, leaving a calling card, finding a way of ensuring respectful attention for the first novel that was going to knock John Fowles into a pile of paperclips. Later still came the lure of hard cash – lit crit paid well in the boom years of the late '80s and early '90s (more of this later) and a sharp operator who reviewed for two or three newspapers and didn't mind the odd hours could make as much as £15,000 a year. Meanwhile, the sheen of punditry could not be ignored – even a book review, after all, may be regarded as a brick in the wall of what is known as 'literary culture.' And finally there is habit. Two thousand volumes in, book reviewing is, like following Norwich City Football Club or watching HBO box sets, something I do, a skill which, up till now, has never forsaken me, a reflexive twitch never to be subdued.

As for those first principles, anyone who launches into print with a 300 word notice of Sadie Blackeye's arresting first novel, *It's Nicer Lying Down*, for the *Cleethorpes Advertiser* will be uncomfortably aware that they have two prospective audiences in view. One is a no doubt exacting posterity, but the second – unless you happen to be writing for a more exalted redoubt like the *TLS* or the *LRB* – is someone who has probably stumbled upon the page by accident, may not be especially interested in literature *per se*, and wants only to know whether the item before them is worth buying or borrowing from a library. All very well imagining that in sending Ms Blackeye's debut down the chute to a well-deserved oblivion you are making a contribution to the culture of your day, but most book reviews are read in horribly mundane circumstances by people wondering if their £16.99 mightn't be better spent. Written in horribly mundane circumstances, too: Anthony Powell's memoirs offer a heartfelt paragraph about the awfulness of having to write round-up reviews for the pre-war *Daily Telegraph*, his defence of books which friends found unreadable being that 'a novel-reviewing job cannot be held down… by writing week after week that the whole depressing batch lack the smallest merit.'

Inevitably, the suspicion that you were barely tolerated by your paymasters worked its effect. The mark of the specimen reviewer, back in the days when I first started taking an interest in them, was an absolute determination to sing for one's supper. As Auberon Waugh, a particular hero of mine, once counselled, the great secret was 'not to ask whether you approve of a book or think it good but to allow yourself to react to it, even if only with exasperation. The key quality in reviewing is not judiciousness or erudition or good taste, least of all is it moderation. It is liveliness of response.' Naturally, there were times when that liveliness degenerated into straightforward stridency. The Friday mornings of my late teens found me keenly awaiting the weekly fiction masterclass that a youthful Peter Ackroyd ran at the back end of *The Spectator*, which specialised in taking serious people a lot less seriously than they wished to be taken, and where the luckless Erica Jong – to cite only one of Ackroyd's punch-bags – was once accused of stuffing herself with clichés in the same way that a scarecrow 'might have to wad himself with pieces of straw and old newspaper…'

The reviewer's task, or so I assured myself on the strength of these exhibition bouts, was a) to cultivate a modest scepticism, b) to assume that nine out of ten novels were scarcely worth noticing, and, above all, c) to impress your personality on the text put before you. All of which, it might be argued, are absolutely the worst qualities anyone wanting to appraise literature in the public prints ought to be displaying, but were, when I set properly to work in the late 1980s, exactly what most literary editors seemed to require. Thirty years later it is difficult to appreciate just how rancorous, how combative and (occasionally) how spiteful were most newspaper books pages in the last days of Mrs Thatcher. It was quite usual, for example, to open the *Observer*'s literary section and discover that all five of the week's novels had been ceremoniously trashed. 'Book reviewing is becoming a blood sport again' *Private Eye*'s anonymous critic (in fact myself) observed in the autumn of 1989 after a bruised and battered Iris Murdoch and her novel *The Message to the Planet* had been borne miserably from the ring.

There were several reasons for this torrent of what in some cases was little more than licensed abuse. Here in the wake of Rupert Murdoch's defeat of the print workers, newspapers were in boom. There was more space for the arts, and the books pages of the day were swiftly colonised by a gang of young reviewers – I was one of them – bent on making names for themselves and causing trouble for its own sake. Additionally, there lurked a suspicion that one or two senior British writers – names mentioned included Kingsley Amis, Margaret Drabble and poor Ms Murdoch – had been getting away with inferior work for rather too long and deserved every rebuke that could be flung at them. In slight mitigation may be advanced the fact that, as the *Independent*'s former literary editor Boyd Tonkin once put it to me, literary culture was robust enough in those times to be able to bear this kind of constant belittling. You could have a little fun with poor Sir Kingsley and his increasingly tortured syntax because both the space and the appetite for these assaults was in abundant supply.

Three decades later, on the other hand, we inhabit a world in which most books are not so much reviewed as endorsed and where it is not uncommon to open, say, the *Guardian Saturday Review* and find that every single item mentioned is being patted on the back. As it happens, there are excellent reasons for this all-round determination (certain truculent ingrates notwithstanding) not to find fault. One of them is the lack of space for reviews, which tends to encourage most editors to take an emollient line. Taxed with simply acclaiming a series of masterpieces, most literary editors will point out that an average of 4,000 books get published every week: why notice the duds? Another is that pressing contemporary urge not to give offence. A third is a welcome awareness of some of the sensitivities that may be trampled on in a culture much keener on inclusiveness and diversity than in the bad old days of Waugh and Ackroyd. A white writer reviewing a black writer, or a middle-aged male Oxford graduate reviewing a book like Kerry Hudson's *Low Born* generally has to start by thinking very hard about motive, stance and a whole raft of prejudices and assumptions of which he may not be fully aware. A fourth, perhaps, is a much more general uneasiness about the whole business of making a judgment in the first place, of having the cheek to lay down the law in a world where the desirability of law-making is being called sharply into question.

The Oxford academic Sophie Ratcliffe recently wrote a letter on these lines to the *TLS* in which, while approving the idea of a rigorous critical climate, she argued that 'The notion that either individually, or as a community, critics are part of an exercise in separating "good" and "bad" books out, like so many sheep and goats, strikes me as utterly bizarre – not to mention arrogant.' My initial reaction to this was straightforward disbelief. Here was an Oxford don with a first-class mind and a roomful of students to educate who seemed suspicious of her own ability to discriminate between merit and its absence. What could be more absurd? On reflection, I see that what Ms Ratcliffe was trying to do was suggest that one of the tasks facing the professional critic is to interrogate his or her subjectivity, to acknowledge that, *pace* Leavis, no one who approaches any cultural artefact is altogether free of bias and that the exposure of these impulses may be one of the things that makes the review worth writing. If Leavis's views on, say, D.H. Lawrence bear reading about, then so, arguably, do the psychological impulses that led him to form them.

All the same, it is important to set Ms Ratcliffe's insistence that we should all be a bit more thoughtful about the positions we take up and the stances we adopt in the context of the way in which most book reviews get written – that is, on the hoof, to a deadline and in the urgent desire to find something worth saying about an object which, *sub specie aeternitatis*, is not likely to enjoy a very long shelf life. Orwell has some sober reflections about the necessity, when reviewing, of finding a spring balance capable of weighing both a flea and an elephant simultaneously. Then there is that urgent need – something I would continue to argue for, however shaky the subjectivity on which most critical judgments rest – to perform the highly desirable task of exposing the works of certain highly acclaimed titans of modern literature to a scrutiny that most critics are rarely prepared to allow them. *Posthumous* re-evaluation, is of course, a wholly different thing, and it is a fact that all the people now queueing up to disparage an Updike or a Mailer tend to have kept their views to themselves while their subjects lived.

But to return to that initial question: why review books? A straight answer might be: to try to understand them better, to encourage readers to understand them better, and also, with Ms Ratcliffe in mind, to understand yourself better. All the same, a certain part of me still experiences a thrill of admiration at the sight of an opinionated young Turk tearing into some grand eminence of the London book world who should know better. I can't help it. You see, it was the way I was brought up.

The Critic, 2019